PRAISE FOR
UNDERDOG NATION

"*Underdog Nation,* Quang X. Pham's incredible underdog journey from Vietnam to America and from the Marines to biotech is a must read!"

—Michael Waltz
National Security Adviser, former Congressman from Florida, bestselling author, and Green Beret combat veteran

"*Underdog Nation* is an essential read for leaders and anyone striving for something *more* in life. Drawing from his incredible journey of overcoming insurmountable odds, Quang X. Pham shares powerful lessons in leadership and resilience. Through practical insights and real-world wisdom, his book serves as both a trusted guide and a source of inspiration for navigating life's inevitable challenges. When you find yourself off course, *Underdog Nation* will be the roadmap to get you back on track."

—Carey D. Lohrenz
former US Navy fighter pilot, CEO, Wall Street Journal bestselling author of Fearless Leadership: High-Performance Lessons from the Flight Deck and Span of Control

"Quang X. Pham's personal story is one of incredible courage and resilience. He has turned his own hardship and pain into a pragmatic framework to achieve success that almost anyone can apply to their own personal and professional lives. A unique and unflinchingly honest approach to separating self-worth from setback, reframing and owning negative results as a way to recalibrate a path to success."

—Holly May
Chief Human Resources Officer of Petco, former CHRO of Walgreens Boots Alliance and Abercrombie & Fitch

"*Underdog Nation* is the patriotic journey of a war refugee who became a Marine Corps pilot, then CEO of a Nasdaq-listed company. Quang X. Pham's definition of success as something driven by effort and results—with relatable life lessons to be read and heard—will resonate with many audiences."

—Alison Levine
Mountaineer and New York Times *bestselling author of* On The Edge

"Twenty years after chronicling his journey from South Vietnam to the Marine Corps in *A Sense of Duty*, Quang X. Pham is back with his astonishing second act. *Underdog Nation* bundles his lifetime of achievements, which includes serving as CEO of a biotech firm that IPO'd, into a practical framework for business and social success that converts life's obstacles into propellant. Inspiring stuff from Pham, who's always a Marine."

—Owen West
Former Assistant Secretary of Defense for Special Operations, retired Goldman Sachs partner, acclaimed author, and Marine combat veteran

UNDERDOG NATION

CHILD REFUGEE | US MARINE | BIOTECH CEO

QUANG X. PHAM

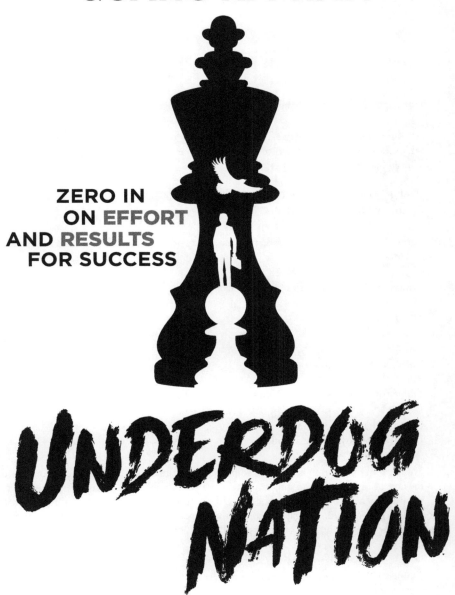

ZERO IN
ON **EFFORT**
AND **RESULTS**
FOR SUCCESS

UNDERDOG NATION

Forbes | Books

Copyright © 2025 by Quang X. Pham.

All rights reserved. No part of this book may be used or reproduced in any manner whatsoever without prior written consent of the author, except as provided by the United States of America copyright law.

Published by Forbes Books, Charleston, South Carolina.
An imprint of Advantage Media Group.

Forbes Books is a registered trademark, and the Forbes Books colophon is a trademark of Forbes Media, LLC.

Printed in the United States of America.

10 9 8 7 6 5 4 3 2 1

ISBN: 979-8-89188-215-7 (Hardcover)
ISBN: 979-8-89188-216-4 (eBook)

Library of Congress Control Number: 2024926391

Cover design by David Taylor.
Layout design by Ruthie Wood.

This custom publication is intended to provide accurate information and the opinions of the author in regard to the subject matter covered. It is sold with the understanding that the publisher, Forbes Books, is not engaged in rendering legal, financial, or professional services of any kind. If legal advice or other expert assistance is required, the reader is advised to seek the services of a competent professional.

Since 1917, Forbes has remained steadfast in its mission to serve as the defining voice of entrepreneurial capitalism. Forbes Books, launched in 2016 through a partnership with Advantage Media, furthers that aim by helping business and thought leaders bring their stories, passion, and knowledge to the forefront in custom books. Opinions expressed by Forbes Books authors are their own. To be considered for publication, please visit **books.Forbes.com**.

For our daughter, Willow.

CONTENTS

ACKNOWLEDGMENTS XI

AUTHOR'S NOTE XIII

INTRODUCTION 1

CHAPTER 1 11
Start with Success

CHAPTER 2 27
The Coincidence of Destiny

AVENUE OF APPROACH 1 47
COMMIT

CHAPTER 3 49
**Love What You Do Until You
Can Do What You Love**

CHAPTER 4 63
Individual Accountability

CHAPTER 5 .77
Be Ready When Your Number Is Called

AVENUE OF APPROACH 2 91
CONFRONT

CHAPTER 6 93
Identifying Barriers

CHAPTER 7 107
Clearing the Path

AVENUE OF APPROACH 3 121
COURSE CORRECT

CHAPTER 8 123
From Loser to Winner

CHAPTER 9 135
Overcoming the Darkest Days

AVENUE OF APPROACH 4 149
BUILD CREDIBILITY

CHAPTER 10 151
Establishing Professional Credibility

CHAPTER 11 165
Navigating Your Identity

CHAPTER 12 179
Aligning Personal Purpose and Company Mission

CONCLUSION 193
The ER Approach in Action

ABOUT THE AUTHOR 199

ACKNOWLEDGMENTS

I would like to thank my editor, Jonathan Jordan, for his fine touches on this book. Nate Best, Forbes Books editorial manager, was extremely helpful, and so were Alison Morse, Publisher Adam Witty, and the entire Forbes Books team for making *Underdog Nation* a reality.

My sweet life partner, Amy, was there to support me through the very early mornings at my desk and weekends of writing and when I needed her most.

Without the encouragement from the late Mike Tharp, a Vietnam veteran and an esteemed journalist, and my American uncle Buck, my writing would have stopped years ago. Mike Hedges of AARP continues to support me, despite our Kentucky/UCLA basketball rivalry arguments over the years. Carey Lohrenz was extremely helpful in sharing her publishing and speaking experience.

Thank you to the investors and shareholders of Cadrenal Therapeutics, who continue to support us in our quest to gain FDA approval for tecarfarin. Our management team and our board of directors are greatly appreciated for their dedication to advancing tecarfarin for patients. Dr. Steve Zelenkofske taught me many nuances of drug development, and I am greatly appreciative of his friendship and patience.

I am especially grateful for John Murphy, also a director, who was the first outside investor in Cadrenal. I had met John through Sawgrass Country Club, where many members are friends and supporters. Jerry

Michaud and Horizon Technology Finance were kind enough to give me another chance with tecarfarin and Cadrenal, and I cannot thank them enough. Dr. Pascal Druzgala and Dr. Peter Milner will forever be credited for inventing tecarfarin. I hope to make their invention an approved drug someday soon for patients still in need. Thanks to Keith Moore and Boustead Securities for taking Cadrenal public during an extremely difficult fundraising environment. Together, we have declared war on warfarin.

Thanks to Wayne Yetter, a Vietnam vet and my first CEO, who supported me during the most difficult days at Espero BioPharma, and Marianne Boskamp, for trusting me enough to license her fine pharmaceutical products from Germany.

My entrepreneurial career got a huge jump start with the $5 million investment by Hummer Winblad Venture Partners, thanks to Ann Winblad, John Hummer, and Dan Beldy. Also thank you to Jeani Delagardelle and Ron Hunt from New Leaf Venture Partners for their funding and support of this first-time underdog CEO. Reide Rosen and D&R Communications saw the potential of MyDrugRep.com and acquired us over a decade ago, and I thank him. Thanks to my UCLA classmate Rod McDermott for believing in me during my brief run for Congress and for supporting Espero BioPharma. My big brother Doug Hamlin, who recruited me into the Marines four decades ago, remains a close friend, confidant, and member guest partner.

Finally, a proud *Semper Fi* to all the US Marines I have befriended and met over the years. You've allowed this underdog to serve with you Devil Dogs, and for that, I am forever indebted.

AUTHOR'S NOTE

I have changed the names of several people in the book to protect their privacy. To my knowledge and memory, everything else is true.

INTRODUCTION

Two decisions in April 1975 would forever alter the course of my life. The first decision was by my father, a senior pilot in the South Vietnamese Air Force. The second was made by my mother, a middle school teacher.

At the time, I was ten years old and had just finished the fifth grade, with French as my second language. All I had ever known was life in a country at war. Like many little boys, I considered my father my role model, my hero. My parents, my three sisters, and I lived on the military air base in Saigon, and he would be with us one day, and then he would go fly missions for several days. But he always came back.

During the last few years of our time in Saigon, the war had quieted down. Though I wasn't aware of it back then, this was because of the Paris Peace Accords signed under President Richard Nixon. On paper, the Vietnam War was supposed to end like it had in Korea—the US and North Vietnamese had agreed to draw a boundary, splitting the country in two. The North Vietnamese agreed they wouldn't invade the South and released prisoners of war like the late Senator John McCain. In exchange, America agreed to completely withdraw troops. But Secretary of State Henry Kissinger's "acceptance of the continued presence of North Vietnamese troops in South Vietnam"[1] would become the ultimate betrayal of an ally.

Unfortunately, this was the quiet before the storm.

All I noticed was that there were fewer and fewer Americans around. The ones I had known best had been military advisors, including a pilot who flew missions with my father.

In the wake of Watergate, the US was shaken. Eyes moved away from Vietnam to the political drama consuming Washington, DC. Nixon secretly visited China, and the Arabs and the Israelis went into full-blown war. And the North Vietnamese knew the US was distracted and decided to test the peace accords.

First, they crossed the border. And the US didn't respond. More American troops left as promised. My father was away for longer periods, and when he was home, his face was lined with worry like I'd never seen. I heard adults around me whisper about their planned escape. Families we knew disappeared in the night, leaving almost everything behind. Something was wrong.

On the night of April 21, my father woke me and my three sisters. "Grab your clothes," he said in a hushed and hurried tone. "We're headed to the airport. You're leaving the country."

Under the cover of darkness, our family of six rode on a Lambretta scooter to the airport with the little we could carry. We had left our dog behind, so surely this would be temporary.

We boarded a US C-130 aircraft piloted by my father's advisor, along with some other families, the fear and despair palpable on their faces. And then my father made the first decision that changed my life.

Only now did the weight of his words hit me. He had said, "We're headed to the airport," so I had assumed we would all be going

---

1   Malcolm W. Brown, "10-Year Rule Ends," *New York Times*, April 22, 1975, https://www.nytimes.com/1975/04/22/archives/10year-rule-ends.html#.

INTRODUCTION

somewhere together. But he had also said, "You're leaving the country," not "We're leaving the country." He stayed behind.

As the plane took off, I couldn't understand why. Among the other families aboard were other South Vietnamese soldiers—men like my father. Why were they leaving with their families while my father did not?

The thought struck me again: *This is temporary. We wouldn't leave Dad and the dog behind if we weren't coming back soon.*

A week later, in a refugee camp on Guam island, we heard the news crackle over the radio. Saigon had fallen. The new South Vietnamese president had surrendered. The war was finally over, and we had lost. South Vietnam was no more. Losers left town. The life I had known for ten years was forever gone.

We had no news of my father. Whether he had lived, been captured, or died—no way for us to know. My mother was left alone with four young children, and now she had a decision to make—where were we to go?

Though my father had learned English from his military training in the US, we knew none. We were bilingual, but in Vietnamese and French. Some of my mother's family had already fled to Paris, so one of our options—the obvious, safe, and logical option—was to join them. At least then we would know the language and have a support system of family already in place to help us resettle.

Instead, my mother decided on America. A week later, we were in the refugee resettlement camp at Fort Chaffee in Arkansas. We might as well have been on another planet. The air was different. The language. The food. The bigger people.

Years later, when I asked my mother why she chose the unknowns of America over France, her answer was simple and direct: "Because I believed you would have more opportunities in America."

3

Turns out, she was right. There would be many opportunities for this new underdog in America.

Nearly forty-eight years later, I would find myself with our team ringing the Nasdaq bell at market close to celebrate the initial public offering (IPO) of my latest venture, Cadrenal Therapeutics. We were the first IPO in over four months, the first biotech IPO of 2023—a company that was reborn from the ashes of my previous startup, which had buckled three years earlier. We were another underdog trying to be the newest darling on Wall Street amid the worst biotech financing climate.

To be clear, this book is not a pure memoir. I've already done that with my first book, *A Sense of Duty*, published by Random House in 2005, detailing the influence of my father on my life and my journey in the US Marine Corps. But the context of going from war to Wall Street in a span of nearly fifty years is essential for the substance of the discussions to follow.

My life has largely been marked as one of being the perpetual underdog. Therefore, it's with nothing but gratitude and awe that I can reflect on the unlikely way I ended up in the US, a country known for loving a good underdog story, and the only country where an underdog can go from surviving to thriving. Although at times, especially during our early years, I must admit I had fears of repatriation whenever bullies yelled at me, "Go back to your own country. Go back to Vietnam!"

There's a lot in life you can't control. If my childhood didn't teach me this enough, then my time in the Marine Corps certainly did. You can have all the best training, the best discipline in the world, the best weapons, but when you get into the combat zone, you don't control which way the wind is blowing smoke into your face. Or when the enemy pulls the trigger. Or when the politicians say enough is enough.

INTRODUCTION

What you *can* control is your approach. In recent years, business and personal development books have made much use of the term *mindset*. But mindset is only one piece of the equation. The best mindset in the world won't help you if you don't pair it with action. And that's what approach is—mindset plus action. Or to put it another way, your efforts.

When you put in the effort, you get results. It's simple cause and effect. And if the results aren't what you want, then you adjust your efforts—you tweak your approach. You keep at it until you achieve your results, your success!

Contrary to popular opinion, you don't need someone telling you which habits to perfect or which leadership skills to implement. "Rah-rah" doesn't lead to results. You've probably already done that. And maybe you found some short-lived success, but eventually, you ended up in the same place as before. Why?

Because most "success advice" out there makes things more complicated than they need to be. Life is complicated enough without bombs going off. So the mission of this book is not to further complicate how you chart a path to professional and personal success—the mission is to simplify it. But you must be decisive.

When I look back at my life, from the decisions my parents made that fateful April, to my choice to join the Marines, to my choice to go into pharmaceutical sales, to my choice to become an entrepreneur, I see that two simple ideas have always been at play:

Effort and Results. ER. And going *back* to the ER.

My efforts have been based on quick decision-making skills like what my parents showed under the immense pressure of losing our country. And then further ingrained in me by Marine training. Quick decision-making spurs on effort. You only get results with effort. It

5

starts the cycle. Because once you have results, then you know how to adjust your efforts.

Look at any underdog, and this has also been their approach, whether they realized it or not. They put in the effort. They looked at the results. And then they adjusted their efforts until they finally achieved the results they wanted.

When you analyze George Washington's military career, you realize he lost more battles than he won. But the battles he won were the most strategic. When you win the right battles, then it changes the results of your losses. You flip your field-of-life position. You measure what matters and recycle those results back into your efforts. That's the heart and soul of *Underdog Nation*.

The term *underdog* has a less-than-savory history. It originally comes from the seedy world of dogfighting, referring to a dog who has lost a fight and, therefore, is considered a bad bet for future fights. My former country South Vietnam was definitely an underdog. And America was definitely an underdog at Sullivan's Island in 1776.

I joined the Marine Corps, which had been an underdog military service (and the smallest) until World War II. The Army and the Navy had wanted to disband our Corps because they saw the Marine Corps as extraneous. But after Marines raised the flag on Iwo Jima, Congress ensured the Marine Corps would exist forever.

Being an underdog means people don't expect much from you—certainly not a success story. You're too much of a risk for them to place their bets on. You're starting from behind. You've got the highest handicap on the golf course. People don't really care about you.

Most people are looking for the "sure thing," the "best bet." They want to back the top dog. So I'll let you in on a little secret: Don't try to be like most people when you are not like most people. Be your underdog self.

INTRODUCTION

Where top dogs expect success, underdogs earn it. The goal of this book is to teach you how to harness the scrappy strength of the underdog through your effort and results. Life is challenging enough—your approach to success doesn't have to be. Embrace—and then unleash—your inner underdog.

Some of the greatest challenges I've faced came from moving to the United States. But also some of the greatest opportunities. I'm grateful for both because they've taught me to apply the approach of the underdog and to transform coincidences into destiny.

During the fall of 1987 when I was starting my Marine officer career, my father was finally freed from the prison war camps where he had been held captive for twelve long years. In 1992, we were finally reunited. So it turns out ten-year-old me was right: "Dad always comes back." And we were able to spend eight more years with him before we lost him to a stroke while he was fighting cancer. My mind often goes to the names of the more than fifty-eight thousand Americans on the Vietnam Wall who never came home. We were extremely fortunate to get our father back.

In many ways, it's this final loss of my father that spurred me on to where I am today in the risky realm of drug development. My current venture, Cadrenal Therapeutics, is an underdog company developing *tecarfarin*, a new blood thinner. We're looking to displace *warfarin*, a drug that was once used as rat poison and labeled as "the most dangerous drug in America"[2] but had been the standard blood thinner for sixty years.

---

2 Charles Ornstein, "Coumadin: 'The Most Dangerous Drug in America,'" *Lexington Herald Leader*, updated July 13, 2015, https://www.kentucky.com/news/local/article44609697.html.

Big Pharma has Eliquis and Xarelto, which makes tecarfarin an underdog drug. But patients with rare cardiovascular conditions need it, and enough physicians will want it available as an option to save lives.

Cardiovascular diseases remain the number one killer worldwide, with heart attacks and strokes being the top culprits. Yet investments in heart drugs are minimal as the FDA's requirements are onerous and make clinical trials lengthy and expensive.

These facts don't deter us at Cadrenal. We keep pushing tecarfarin forward with our efforts.

The underlying purpose for Cadrenal is that I've always wondered if my father's stroke could have been mitigated through the availability of another blood thinner. While it's not worth fixating on this hypothetical, the thought inspired me to do what I can to prevent the same pain for others.

Persistence is key for underdogs. After all, given the stringent (but necessary) requirements for FDA clinical trials, most drugs fail and money is lost. It's definitely a business where an underdog mentality is not only an asset but a prerequisite. Despite these obstacles, we're proof that people love a good underdog story.

Though I can only speak to my own experience, there's enough variety in those experiences to provide ample examples of how the underdog approach has served me well. Not many people can come to the table with the same profile:

- War refugee/immigrant
- Marine pilot and combat veteran
- Top-producing salesperson at major pharmas
- Founder of multiple startups—a mixture of successes and a failure

INTRODUCTION

The principles taught in this book have proven true across all of these phases of my life, so I have great confidence you can adapt and adopt them to your situation.

A huge piece of my love for the United States is our own history as an underdog nation. In 1776, a scrappy group of thirteen colonies had the guts to go toe-to-toe with the greatest superpower in the world. And we won. It's the *U* that I see in USA—*United* ... and *Underdog*.

Even though the United States has been a top dog in the world since the end of World War II, we have continued our history of supporting the underdogs. We did it in Korea. And again in Vietnam. And again in the Gulf War. We're certainly not perfect—look no further than Vietnam for proof. But no human or nation is perfect.

Perfection is an impossible goal. The approach of the underdog is continuous improvement—becoming better than you were yesterday. Sometimes you'll fail. Sometimes you'll succeed. The point is that you always get off the floor and rise again. Your goals don't depend on anyone else when you're an underdog. You define success by your own terms—and then you put in the effort to drive the results you want.

Most of the world is looking for a shortcut to success. In the process, they're making it far more complicated than they need to. And for the most part, this mentality of "hacks" and "tricks" and "nuggets" leads to disappointment. Maybe that's where you are today—feeling jaded, stuck, left out, and lost.

If so, consider this book an invitation to a different path—an invitation to become a citizen of the Underdog Nation. You don't need another mindset shift or an expensive life coach. What you need is to determine what success means to you and then align your effort and results to that definition. You need the ability to make quick decisions and the willingness to adjust your efforts based on the results. Take yourself to the ER!

UNDERDOG NATION

What you need is the heart and soul of the underdog. It's something you'll have to cultivate for yourself. You'll have to plant the seeds and water them. But my hope is this book will serve as your almanac, your flight plan, so you can make the most of your effort, drive the results you need, and take hold of the success you've been looking for.

Ringing the closing bell at Nasdaq to celebrate our IPO in 2023 (Author's Collection)

CHAPTER 1

Start with Success

Our Marine aircrew on the last day of the Gulf War, 1991 (Author's Collection)

February 27, 1991 is burned into my memories. Under the leadership of Saddam Hussein, Iraq had invaded Kuwait seven months earlier—a force of one hundred thousand against Kuwait's twenty-thousand-man army. It wasn't a fair fight. Most wars don't begin as fair fights.

By all accounts, the Kuwaiti forces fought valiantly, but around 4,200 fell in battle. The emir of Kuwait was forced to flee after a final broadcast pleading for help before Kuwait Radio was silenced on the morning of August 3, 1990.

With the Kuwaiti forces battered and bruised and the Iraqi occupation firmly established, Hussein declared Kuwait conquered, proclaiming it was a province of Iraq, and immediately set out to wipe out Kuwait's identity by renaming its cities. The situation was bleak.

Kuwait was an underdog nation, captive and helpless. But it had oil—and a lot of it. Iraqi troops conducted campaigns of fear across the nation's villages—pillaging, raping, killing.

The story felt too familiar. The first ten years of my life were spent in Saigon. Except Saigon didn't exist anymore (and had little oil). In the same way Hussein was erasing Kuwait's identity, Saigon had been renamed Ho Chi Minh City when North Vietnamese forces marched in on April 30, 1975. By that time, our family was already in a refugee camp on Guam, listening to the death of our beloved South Vietnam over BBC radio as if it were a sports broadcast.

I knew all too well what it was like to be an underdog—to lose a national identity. So when our Marine unit was called into action as part of the first rescue team to head to Kuwait, it wasn't just duty that compelled me. It was a deep sense that I needed to help change the story for a fellow underdog. As a US Marine, I needed to be in the fight.

Operation Desert Storm began on January 17—and now our helicopter unit was being called up to go in. We were briefed for the mission: "Get to the landing zone where our fellow Marines are under fire and pull out the wounded." Our mission was simple: in zone, on time.

Two CH-46E Sea Knight helicopters were to fly in, two pilots assigned to each, two aircrewmen/door gunners and a medical corpsman. All of us were first-timers when it came to warfare, but we still had to be ranked for the mission. I was the most junior officer and pilot, flying copilot in the second helicopter (or Dash-2), on the fourth day of the ground war.

You can be briefed on combat missions until you're blue in the face, but nothing quite prepares you for the real thing. The Iraqi forces had set fire to the oil fields, so as we flew in, the sky was filled with thick black smoke, obscuring our line of sight.

We were using GPS to navigate, long before the technology found its way into civilian life, but it wasn't as accurate as today. We were flying fast and low over power lines, in and out of fires.

At one point, I checked our bearing—and it seemed off. Way off. As the bottom rung of a very short ladder, a part of me was hesitant to speak. Wouldn't the lead chopper already know the bearing was off? Was there a reason for this that I didn't know?

Some might have chosen to stay quiet, but that was never my style. Lives were on the line.

"We're going to the left by thirty degrees," I told the helicopter aircraft commander (HAC).

"Q, are you sure?"

"I'm positive. We need to call the section leader."

Some quick radio chatter and the lead helicopter confirmed I was right—we were off course by a full thirty degrees, which they hadn't yet detected. We course corrected, made it to Kuwait International Airport, our target zone, and airlifted out an injured Marine and four wounded Iraqi soldiers.

Had I stayed silent, had I questioned my own authority, who knows what might have happened. We could have ended up in enemy fire. We could have arrived at the zone too late, and lives could have been lost. But we'll never know because of my simple decision to speak up even though I was the most junior member of the team.

I'm not saying this to pat myself on the back but to make a simple point:

Without effort, you have no results. And without results, you don't know how to adjust your efforts. The two feed off each other. But neither will do you much good if you can't define success. You have to be strong. You need to take the risk. You must speak up.

Define Success First

$E=mc^2$ may be the most famous equation in all the world, but do you know what it actually means?

In short, Albert Einstein's equation teaches that energy and mass are interchangeable. What Einstein does beautifully with the equation is take a complex subject and express it in the simplest terms. The equation explains why you feel warmth from a fire and why the stars shine.

But what stands out to me the most is how the equation is written—it starts with the answer. He could have written it as $mc^2=E$, but he didn't. He put Energy first because that's what he wanted to define. And then he reverse engineered to determine the rest of the equation.

Einstein himself was an underdog. He wasn't a beacon of academia during childhood. In fact, he dropped out of school at the age of fifteen. His teachers expected nothing from him. Even in university, he was fired from multiple tutoring jobs and had a reputation for offending his professors by cutting class to study on his own. At the time he penned the paper behind $E=mc^2$, he was working as a lowly patent clerk. And yet he went on to win a Nobel Prize and become the most famous scientist of his era, if not of all time.

The key to Einstein's success wasn't just his talent. It was his determination to define success on his own terms. He didn't let his teachers define it for him. By defining success for himself, he could focus on the efforts that would yield the results he wanted—not what others wanted.

The equation for success is similar. You could write it as $S=er3$, where S represents "Success," e represents "efforts," and r^3 represents "results." Why are results cubed? Admittedly, I'm bending the rules of mathematics here, but it's because results are three-dimensional. They are the tangible evidence of your efforts and determine your future efforts.

Unfortunately, this approach is diametrically opposed to how most of us have been taught, both in school and in the workplace. We have been taught to let others define our success, whether through a grade, credential, or some other standard. In your career, success is often defined through promotions. So when you are passed over for a promotion or given a lateral move, no wonder you feel like a failure.

Life has taught me that your best approach is often to start by assuming success. My golf buddies tease me over this. I frequently get jibes of, "Q, you think you're always going to win, don't you?" To which I smile and say, "I do."

My time in the Marines reinforced this belief. So did my career in sales. And this approach has served me well in entrepreneurship.

This may sound counterintuitive, but underdogs go into the fight assuming success. And a primary reason underdogs succeed is because they have formed their own definition of success, no matter how anyone else defines it.

Look no further than *Rocky*.

The *Rocky* franchise has earned over $1.7 billion, but it started out as the underdog of all underdog movies. When Sylvester Stallone wrote the script, he only had $106 in his bank account, no car, and was even considering selling his dog since he couldn't afford dog food.

When movie producers Irwin Winkler and Robert Chartoff became interested in his script, they offered an incredible $350,000 for the script over fifty years ago.

For context, the average spec script sells for about $110,000 in today's market, assuming you have some prior writing experience. Most people in Stallone's situation would have immediately asked for the pen and run to the bank. But Sylvester Stallone isn't most people. He had a different definition for success.

He refused to sell the script unless the producers agreed to let him star in the movie. This ultimatum put them in a bind. They loved the script, but they had been planning to pick a star who could guarantee ticket sales—someone like Ryan O'Neal or Burt Reynolds. Not a no-name writer-actor with a hungry dog.

The producers wanted the script badly enough they finally agreed to let Stallone star, but in return, the studio slashed the budget from $2 million to $1 million. Apparently, Stallone's underdog spirit was infectious because Winkler and Chartoff ended up mortgaging their houses to add $100,000 to the budget.[3]

The movie instantly struck a chord, and their bet paid off. *Rocky* earned over $200 million at the box office when it was released in 1976, and Stallone became a household name. The following year, the movie continued its underdog streak, winning the Academy Award for Best Picture despite competition from the star-studded film *Network*.

Likewise, the character of Rocky Balboa has a different definition for success. In a key scene of the movie, he says, "All I wanna do is go the distance. Nobody's ever gone the distance with Creed, and if I can go that distance, you see, and that bell rings and I'm still standin',

---

[3] IMDb, "Rocky—Trivia," IMDb.com, accessed October 9, 2024, https://www.imdb.com/title/tt0075148/trivia/.

CHAPTER 1: **START WITH SUCCESS**

I'm gonna know for the first time in my life, see, that I wasn't just another bum from the neighborhood."[4]

Even though Apollo Creed is named the winner of the fight at the end of the movie, Rocky doesn't bat his bloodied eyes. His head is held high, a champion in his own mind because he fulfilled his own definition of success by staying on his feet through fifteen grueling rounds, the underdog facing the top dog.

The famous training montage of the film shows Rocky's efforts to achieve the results: stamina, strength, and balance. As he achieves these results, his efforts are compounded—eventually bringing him to his own definition of success—going the distance.[5]

Your first step in success is to follow the path of Einstein and his equation, the path of Stallone and his character Rocky Balboa—define success first. If you let others define success for you, it becomes a moving target. You will either never hit it, or even if you do, it will never bring you the satisfaction promised.

Most people are going about it all wrong. They're starting with effort, working their tails off but with no clear view of what they are working toward. Then they are disappointed with the results, feel lost, and all too often, settle for becoming less than their best. You don't have to be most people.

When you have defined success on your terms, you can complete the equation by taking more ownership over both your effort and your results. You'll create your own underdog narrative. You'll write the story no one expects—but the one you have earned.

---

[4] *Rocky*, directed by John G. Avildsen (1976; West Hollywood, CA: United Artists).

[5] Of course, my favorite Stallone film is *First Blood*, where he played John Rambo, an underdog Vietnam veteran on the run from the police.

The Underdog Approach

Much of recent business and leadership literature has focused on the importance of mindset. The concept has been so overwrought that it's become white noise.

Don't get me wrong—mindset plays an essential role in defining your own success. But we have put too much emphasis on it—mostly emotional—at the expense of real action.

Mindset doesn't win battles. Mindset doesn't grow businesses. Mindset doesn't persuade investors. Mindset doesn't earn promotions. It is a factor, but it is only effective when it becomes action.

Therefore, when considering the formula for success, I realized that discussing mindset alone would be incomplete. You can have the best mindset in the world, but if it never leads to action, then you'll never get anywhere. You're better off taking action, even if your mindset isn't exactly where it should be yet. Because through the results of your actions, you can reshape your mindset. *Mindsetting is just dreaming.*

What sets underdogs apart from everyone else is their willingness to take action and risk. David didn't simply think he could defeat Goliath. He picked up stones and a slingshot. Sylvester Stallone didn't simply think he could be a movie star. He insisted on playing the lead role at the risk of losing the deal. Daniel "Rudy" Ruettiger didn't simply think he could play for Notre Dame football. He worked his tail off in both the classroom and the field to earn a spot on the team.

Americans in general don't root for underdogs who fail or lose. No one cares about the Davids and Rudys if they don't win. We don't love underdogs for their mindset. We love them for their actions. *Underdogs take the first punch. They are the doers.*

Therefore, the framework we'll be diving into throughout the book is what I call the underdog approach. And rather than complicate success, it relies on the simple equation already introduced:

Success = Effort x Results[3]

Effort is what you can control. It's the discipline and actions you take every day to work toward your definition of success.

Results are all about the analysis, looking at three dimensions:

- What went right that I should keep doing?
- What went wrong that I can improve upon?
- What should I try next?

The answers to those three questions multiply your effort. So even when your efforts lead to different results than you hoped for, you can still make progress. You can adjust your approach on your path to the success you've defined.

In aviation, the word *approach* refers to the stage of flight when the aircraft descends and maneuvers to land. In any approach, the pilot has to take action in two directions—lateral and vertical.

Lateral refers to the aircraft's longitudinal position in relation to the landing zone. Or put another way, lateral is asking, "Am I landing evenly?" Things can go literally sideways quickly when your lateral angle is off.

Vertical refers to the distance between the aircraft and the landing zone, also considering the rate of descent. Come in too fast and it doesn't matter how good your lateral approach is—you'll crash and burn, especially during a dark night on the ominous Indian Ocean and its rolling seas.

You can see lateral and vertical as stand-ins for effort and results. The two not only work together for a successful landing; they multiply each other. Effort compounds results. Results compound effort.

Though the underdog approach is simple to describe, there are many ways in which it can play out, which is what the rest of this book will explore. In particular, we'll take a look at four nuanced approaches:

APPROACH 1: COMMIT

This approach is all about committing to excellence by focusing on the right effort. You can't run the Boston Marathon well simply by running seven days a week. You have to have a plan, practice, and execute. Committing is not only about dedication but about yearning to look for the winning approach as you learn and grow.

APPROACH 2: CONFRONT

This approach is about confronting your obstacles. The Underdog Nation is filled with challenges and roadblocks. If you don't yet have the skills necessary to overcome them, then you have to define the efforts you need to take. Find your gaps and then strategically fill them.

APPROACH 3: COURSE CORRECT

You'll have to deviate from your plan at some point, whether because of external forces or because you make mistakes. Success is not achieved through perfection. It's achieved through making constant course corrections. Expect failures along the way so you can develop backup plans. Many companies have shut down because they didn't have a plan B. One-trick ponies may have fast starts, but they don't make it to the finish line.

APPROACH 4: CREDIBILITY BUILDING

There are two types of successful people in the world: those with traditional credentials and those with street cred. In Underdog Nation, we favor the latter. You may not have the "right" résumé or background or education. You may feel like you've wasted years in the wrong field or profession, but I'm here to tell you that you haven't. You can always build off of where you are and acquire the credibility you need. Take the correct turn at the fork on the career and life road.

All four of these approaches are driven by a focus on E and R—Effort and Results. And you can't spell *underdog* without *E* and *R* right at the center. By centering Effort and Results, you can unleash your inner underdog to win success on your own terms.

Effort and Results

Many Americans didn't excuse Vietnam as a loss because the United States fulfilled their end of the Paris Peace Accords by withdrawing troops as promised. But due to the political pressures and lack of public support for the war, the US chose not to re-engage with the North Vietnamese when they broke the treaty.

The US decided it had already given as much effort as it would in light of the results. Enough was enough. That guilt became the true Vietnam syndrome for nearly two decades.

The unfortunate result was a loss for our family and people. It wasn't for lack of effort on our part, though that wasn't the narrative spun for decades. Fifty years later, I still hear the same rhetoric repeated at times: "They didn't even try to defend their country. The South Vietnamese were lazy. They expected America to do everything for them."

But the numbers don't support this narrative. As mentioned in my first book, *A Sense of Duty*, nearly 245,000 South Vietnamese died defending our former country—around four times the amount of US deaths. And after the war, another 65,000 political victims were executed, and thousands more died in the so-called "reeducation camps" like the ones my father spent twelve years in.

In the equation of success, we have to face the fact that there is a clear relationship between your effort and your decisions. Good effort alone is not enough. It's about the *right* effort. Because the right effort leads to optionality. The right effort gives you more choices. And with more choices, you can make better decisions and have better outcomes—sometimes different from the ones you originally pursued.

Decisions are made from your collective experiences and confidence in your own abilities—that is, determination. No one wakes up with fully formed determination. Rather, it's a buildup process. However, you can accelerate determination with one simple decision:

Doing what people say you can't do.

Which brings us back to the underdog approach. You can always find people who want to tell you what you cannot do. Not all of them are your enemies either. A good number will be well-meaning loved ones who believe they are looking out for your best interests.

People said a Vietnamese refugee couldn't become a Marine pilot. So I did it anyway. People said I couldn't succeed in sales without years of experience. So I did it anyway. People said I couldn't be the CEO of a startup without previous fundraising experience. So I did it anyway. Over twenty publishers rejected my first book. Yet I wrote it anyway.

When you're letting other people define success for you, you'll never know what you're truly capable of. But when you define success for yourself, then you gain more autonomy over the effort and results. You increase your choices. You enhance your decision-making.

Let's not pretend this means everything magically works out. There will always be factors outside your control. You are human and will make mistakes. But even these can be reframed as results that shape your future efforts.

Without results, it doesn't matter how much effort you pour in. The math has to add up. The results are the feedback required to decide when to double down, when to pivot, or when to retreat. Even Marines have had to retreat and establish defensive positions, as in Korea from the Chosin Reservoir and in Vietnam at Khe Sanh. They pulled back and recalculated. When the math doesn't add up, then you take a hard look at whether you defined success accurately. You don't always have to go on a frontal assault.

The Marines taught me how to calculate risk, how to mission plan, and how to adapt to change. Not UCLA, not business school. And not Harvard. Most importantly, the Marine Corps taught me how to plan for the most important functions: action in the objective area, closing the deal, selling when it's not hot, and raising money during the toughest times.

The biggest lesson from my military service was to simplify the decision-making process through a "go/no-go" set of criteria. There was no third option to muddy the water. We utilized a decision-making matrix and then always had a backup plan if things went south. This is what gave me the confidence to speak up on that first mission to Kuwait, and it's given me the confidence in every career decision I've made since.

In your career, not all decisions will be life-or-death scenarios like in the military. But all decisions you make require a combination of two factors:

- Experience (i.e., your efforts)
- Risk assessment (i.e., the results, including potential results)

Where you lack experience, you can turn to the people you admire who are ten steps ahead of you. When we flew into the thick smoke of warfare, we were all new. No one in our unit had ever flown in a combat situation. But our CO (commanding officer) was a Vietnam veteran himself and was able to impart his experience to us.

Some may call these individuals role models. I prefer to call them *Admirables*. They're the people you admire specifically because they embody a version of the success you have defined. The Admirables are key to finding the path you need to be on—and also the path you should avoid. The late General Colin Powell was my first Admirable. He had served in Vietnam twice, was selected as a White House Fellow, and became the Chairman of the Joint Chiefs of Staff.

When I entered the Marine Corps, I was undecided whether it would be my forever career. My superiors thought I should consider becoming a career Marine after I was selected to be a general's aide-de-camp. This gave me a front-row seat to what a military career could lead to. I was able to "borrow" the general's experience by seeing his day-to-day responsibilities.

The experience helped me realize I didn't want to wait twenty-five years to have that level of decision-making authority. The general's experience gave me insight into my results—I had to recognize the time had come for me to make my exit and pursue other opportunities, to determine a new definition of success for myself.

If you don't know someone directly who can advise you through experience, you have plenty of other resources you can turn to. When I was getting into sales, I sought out the profiles of successful salespeople I admired. I read their books, studied their methods.

Likewise, when I took the leap into entrepreneurship, I sought out the profiles of entrepreneurs I admired. Fred Smith, the founder of FedEx and a Marine Vietnam veteran, stood out. His Yale professor had given him a C for his overnight air delivery business plan, and in true underdog fashion, he executed the business plan anyway after serving his country. My biotech *Admirable* is Bob Duggan, a California surfer who never graduated from college, but became a multi-billionaire by investing in underdogs like Pharmacyclics and Summit Therapeutics. His success shows you don't need a Ph.D., or even a college education, to make money in the complex world of biotechnology.

You need to constantly take yourself to the ER. Not the emergency room, but look at the Effort and Results that will fulfill your personal equation for success. Learn how to reflect on where you've been, where you are, and where you want to be. Only then can you start with success and reverse engineer the Effort and Results you need. You will come across opportunities and people who never crossed your mind previously.

Along the way, you'll have missteps. You'll need a backup plan. You'll need to course correct. If you're consistently taking yourself to the ER, you'll improve at self-diagnosing without dialing 911 or hiring a career coach.

If you're now realizing that the gnawing sense of dissatisfaction is a result of letting others define success for you, then let me encourage you: no experience is wasted.

Remember, most people are going about it backward. They are pouring all their energy into their efforts and disappointed with the results because they don't have their own definition of success. Don't be most people. Start with success. It will be your compass to the right effort and the right results.

Reflaction—Identify Your Admirables

As mentioned before, mindset is not enough on its own. Nor is effort enough on its own. You must combine them through action. Therefore, each chapter, I want to leave you with a reflaction. And no, that's not a typo. Reflactions are where reflections meet actions. They are the brief before the mission.

In the spirit of the underdog, we don't want to complicate the process. We want to find one practical step to take on the road to success.

Therefore, your first assignment is to find one Admirable and study their profile. Hopefully you have an Admirable in your life who closely embodies the trajectory you want to follow. You can borrow their experience to determine your efforts. You can learn from their mistakes to complete your risk assessment. Reach out to them and find a time to talk.

And if you don't know someone personally, your action step is to do some research. Find an Admirable on LinkedIn and look at their history and the steps they took. Find every article you can about them on Google and document how they achieved success. Follow them on social media, engage with their content, read their biographies, attend their keynotes.

If you can't define success for yourself yet, finding your Admirables is a great place to start. Then you have a living framework to study and bring clarity to the ER you need for a fulfilling and profitable life.

CHAPTER 2

The Coincidence of Destiny

A thin line separates destiny from coincidence.
—T. J. STILES, PULITZER PRIZE–WINNING AUTHOR

I almost never met my dad.

While my mother was pregnant with me, my father was flying a joint mission of South Vietnamese and US Marines in Operation Shufly. While engaging in battle, my father's propeller-driven Skyraider bomber was shot down, and he found himself stranded in an area of the jungle overrun by North Vietnamese Army soldiers.

Left there, he would have certainly been captured and killed early in the Vietnam War. Instead, a US Marine helicopter pilot spotted the burning wreckage and, despite the danger to himself and his crew, made a snap decision to rescue my father.

When my father was finally released from the prison camps and came to the US in 1992, I had just returned from my second deployment to the Persian Gulf as a Marine helicopter pilot. We flew the composite squadron of sixteen helicopters, did a flyover of the base, and then landed. There he was, waiting for me after seventeen long years, after I'd believed he was long gone or dead.

Later on, when I was working on my first book, I was going through some tape recordings and handwritten notes given to me by a journalist who had interviewed my father about his time in the South Vietnamese Air Force. In one of my father's notes, he recalled his thoughts as he watched me fly in and saw the tail codes on the helicopters, speaking directly to me through the note:

"It was either simple coincidence or you may call it destiny. You're in the same Marine unit that I flew support for and was rescued by in the early days of the war."

Coincidence? Or destiny?

Back in Vietnam, my mother had been a sixth-grade teacher where teaching was a highly revered profession unlike in the US, where I see most teachers taken for granted. After leaving the temporary refugee camp on Guam, we were initially enrolled in an English as a Second Language program to learn English from a US Vietnam vet. Unfortunately, his Vietnamese was so poor and confusing we made no progress, and the school quickly ended the program.

Though she didn't speak English yet, either, Mom knew we would need the language proficiency if we were to have any kind of chance in the US. She went out and brought home some English books with pictures of a grown bear and her cubs.

"I don't know what those words are," she said, pointing to a page. "But just copy them over and over."

As it turned out, some of those words I copied over and over were *the little bears and the little bruins.* Later on, I was accepted into UCLA, whose team name is the Bruins.

Coincidence? Or destiny?

CHAPTER 2: **THE COINCIDENCE OF DESTINY**

My decision to leave the Marines and take up a career in pharmaceutical sales might be seen as coincidence. After all, it wasn't a career I had spent time investigating. Big Pharma simply had informational booths at a career fair specifically for junior officers transitioning out of active duty. In short, the challenge and earning potential appealed to me.

And yet, that single decision is what put me on the path to where I am today, developing a revolutionary but underdog drug that could have possibly saved my father's life when that stroke took him from us in the midst of cancer treatment.

Coincidence? Or destiny?

A thousand separate events completely outside of my control led to us leaving Vietnam, from my father's rescue in the jungle to political upheaval happening in Washington, DC, to corruption in Saigon.

Every day, a thousand coincidences are happening outside of your control, and you can either see them as a hindrance to overwhelm you—or as a hurdle to overcome. When you choose the latter view, then coincidences are no longer happenstances, but they can be harnessed for the destiny you want.

Life is filled with so-called coincidences. But when you start with a vision for success, aligned with the right effort and results, those coincidences become the building blocks for destiny. Don't play the blame game, which often leads to excuses, bitterness, and resentment.

You don't have to tell me twice that not every South Vietnamese kid who came to America ended up the way I did. We came to this country with the same setbacks—maybe more, given my mother was on her own and we had no language skills. But through her bootstrapping spirit, her underdog determination to not wait for others to decide our fate, she took coincidence into her hands and shaped a destiny for us. After all, millions of immigrants have come to America with similar challenges over the course of our history and led meaningful lives.

The one educational asset we had was that we were three years ahead in mathematics—and math is its own language. So we were able to coast along comfortably in math while we acquired the language skills. By our second year in the US, we were conversational. A year later, we began learning Spanish since US colleges didn't recognize Vietnamese as a second language in their applications. *Yo hablo español también.*

Displacement as a refugee was a coincidence, an unfortunate result of all the decisions outside of our control. But from that displacement, we learned the ability to improvise, adapt, adopt, and overcome way earlier in our lives. It created a foundation for everything the Marines would teach me later.

Adapt and Adopt

When everything bad that could happen to you has already happened, what do you do next? In a span of hours, we had lost our freedom, home, father, and cultural identity—so I don't need any more angry voters and politicians to lecture me about "losing our country." Most Americans don't know what that actually feels like. We literally were left with just the clothes on our backs, with 150,000 enemy soldiers and tanks closing in. Anything good that happened from then on had to come from our own efforts.

That's not to say we didn't have help. Though I've since learned there were people against the decision, President Gerald Ford was able to get a relief bill through Congress to make sure South Vietnamese refugees could be resettled in the US, so long as they were sponsored by American citizens.

CHAPTER 2: **THE COINCIDENCE OF DESTINY**

In that regard, we won the "refugee lottery" when we were sponsored by a family in California and later granted citizenship. Many other families ended up in France or Canada. And while those are fine nations in their own right, hindsight has taught me that we would never have had the same opportunities.

Some families couldn't cope with the change to a new environment, though. Some chose to return to Vietnam and accept life under the winning Communist regime.

When you're facing a sudden disruptive change—personally or professionally—you have to think on your feet and adapt. The same DNA you had before won't work anymore. You've got to change to your new environment if you're going to survive. That's the example my mother showed when she chose for us to go to the US instead of France. It wasn't a decision of convenience. It was calculated. And it turned out to be the correct one.

Adaptation is rooted in survival. No one adapts in the midst of a comfortable environment. So when coincidence comes your way and disrupts the status quo, you have to make a choice—right or left, up or down. You often won't find much gray area because indecision itself is a decision.

This was one of the most valuable lessons early on with the Marines. As a college grad, I was already positioned to become a second lieutenant *if* I graduated from Officer Candidates School (OCS) at Quantico, Virginia. My trainer's eyes were fixed on mine during a field problem exercise—all of which were based on Vietnam-era combat scenarios. I was frozen, thinking hard—what if I made the wrong call and Marines were killed?

"Right or wrong, make a decision, Lieutenant," he barked.

In the heat of battle, a hundred "coincidences" are being fired at you nonstop. You can't be paralyzed. You have to make a decision fast, right or wrong. The Marine mentality is that action is always better than inaction. If you find out you made the wrong decision, you learn from it and adapt to your new circumstances for the next decision.

When I became an entrepreneur, this approach to decision-making immediately set me apart. We would hear from potential partners, "You don't have to make a decision today." But during the peak of the dot-com era, I knew we'd have to act fast or we'd get passed. We wouldn't be able to adapt fast enough to survive. Industry experts told me it was impossible to do an IPO in 2022 but I ignored their warnings anyway and did it.

Meanwhile, corporate America was—and still is—fixated on modeling, spending, taking calculated risk, reaching consensus, and overanalyzing the data. Entrepreneurialism is much more like being dropped into a combat zone without an abundance of cash.

Once you adapt, only then do you have the chance to *adopt*. And that means to *assimilate*. With adoption, you start making choices not from a necessity to survive, but from the opportunity to thrive.

The tricky part about thriving is that while you get to define what it means to you, you may still face some natural limitations. Thanks to the bills pushed through Congress, my family and I were eventually given citizenship and found a small apartment on the poor side of Oxnard, California, *just a little north of Malibu.*

Our neighborhood was kind of run down but ethnically diverse, fondly called *the 'hood*. Back in Vietnam, I had been surrounded by just Vietnamese faces. But now I was surrounded by white people, Mexicans, Black people, other Asians—a true melting pot. At first, everyone assumed we were Chinese and that I was Bruce Lee Jr. Once people learned we were actually Vietnamese, they would frown with confusion and ask, "What are you doing here? I thought we were at war with you people."

CHAPTER 2: **THE COINCIDENCE OF DESTINY**

Since we didn't live in Little Saigon, we were suddenly faced with choices about what adopting our new home country would look like. When the paperwork came in, we had the option of anglicizing our names. Many refugees did so, knowing it would be easier for non-Vietnamese people to pronounce their names: *Bobby Nguyen. Julie Tran.*

But my mother chose not to. We would keep our birth names. To this day, I'm grateful for her decision and that I wasn't renamed Charlie or Victor Charles Pham.

Mom was also a realist, though, and knew we had to assimilate if we were to thrive. So she established a simple rule for us: "When you're at home, you speak Vietnamese. Outside, speak English." And she never once said anything about being a new single mom in America. She had to adopt her new reality.

As I worked on my language skills and interacted with other children in the neighborhood, I saw early on how sports were a big part of American life. In 1976, I decided to try out for the local Little League baseball team even though I didn't know the game at all. I wanted to belong.

While I'll save the full story for later on, the first game ended with me missing a fly ball to right field and the ball striking me in the chest. Everyone laughed. By the next year, I had unleashed my inner underdog and made the winning hit in the championship game.

Throughout the rest of my school years, sports became the space where I could thrive. Sports allowed me to adopt my new homeland and assimilate into American life. Though I had lost a huge part of my identity, I now had the opportunity to develop a new one. I wanted to be on a team, a winning team.

You get to do the same in whatever context you find yourself. However, when most people are faced with life's coincidences, they either give up or they remain in survival mode forever. They retreat to the comforts of what they know. Underdogs don't. Underdogs look at the effort and results they need to thrive.

A thriver never wants a handout. You thrive through your efforts. You have to adopt the attitude and behaviors that will get you there, even when others might not understand, especially those who look and talk like you.

During my early years, I was sometimes criticized by other Vietnamese refugees for becoming too Americanized, because of how I dressed and how I spoke, and even for dating a white girl. And yet some of those criticizing me were the ones who had chosen to anglicize their names.

We were never going to fit in fully with any crowd. We could never feel fully American because we weren't even like other immigrants we knew. We were refugees. We hadn't come to the US purely by choice. It felt like a label that would follow us forever.

But we also didn't feel fully Vietnamese. Since Mom was on her own, we weren't part of "the joy luck club." Dad had been left behind, and so no doubt there were whispers and assumptions about why.

This taught me an early valuable lesson—you can never make everyone happy. If you try to, not only will you fail, but you'll also be allowing someone else to define success for you. Even if you manage to make them happy, you won't be. That's not success. That's a cage.

You don't have to adopt the same choices as others, even when their story is similar to yours. You may take inspiration and insights from others, such as your Admirables, but you still have to recognize the set of coincidences in your life are different from theirs. You still have to chart your own destiny. You may find help like we did, but no one else will *do* it for you.

When you're adept at both adapting and adopting, you get to escape the victim mentality that keeps most people fixated on their circumstances instead of living out their purposes. You stop making excuses. You get to be the underdog, wielding both effort and results as your destiny takes shape.

Transforming Coincidences into Destiny

Coincidences are totally outside your control. You don't get to choose your family. You don't get to choose which country you're born into. Coincidences are often the results of someone else's choices, someone else's efforts.

But the real question isn't coincidence versus destiny. Rather, it's more about how you take coincidence and transform it into destiny. How?

By going back to the ER. Examine yourself through your effort and results.

Destiny is directly connected to your definition of success. It's knowing your direction so that you're ready when your number's called.

For instance, I wasn't even supposed to go overseas for Operation Desert Shield (before Operation Desert Storm). Our peer group wasn't getting called up to go since we were fresh out of flight school. But an assigned pilot's wife fell ill, so he returned home and that squadron needed a replacement pilot.

Our commanders could have assigned someone. They could have made it a matter of coincidence and flipped a coin. Instead, they asked for volunteers. The other guys in my unit all assumed they would eventually be deployed as a unit. But me? I didn't want to leave it up to coincidence. If there was going to be a war, then I needed to be there. So I volunteered and flew by myself from Southern California to Saudi Arabia to join my first combat squadron.

Much of my decision to join the Marines was directly tied to the destiny I wanted for myself. As a kid, I wanted to be a military pilot like my dad. But when we South Vietnamese lost our war and our country, I thought that dream was over. The Marine Corps represented a chance to transform the coincidences of my past into destiny. The Marine who recruited me was Captain Doug Hamlin, who went on to become CEO of the embattled and controversial National Rifle Association (NRA) in 2024. He became the big American brother I never had.

You could look at the original pilot's wife getting sick as a coincidence. And perhaps it was. But me being ready in time—and the decision to volunteer—was destiny. The war was over within weeks, and my former unit stayed home, whereas I became a war veteran, fulfilling the destiny I had once dreamed of as a child. And paying back my lottery American citizenship.

That's where effort comes in. If you haven't put in the effort ahead of time to be ready, then you'll miss your chance. You'll remain a victim of coincidence. You won't get off the bench.

I've seen this play out time after time throughout my life—from losing my homeland, assimilating into American culture, going to war, and even working in sales and entrepreneurship. With a focus on effort and results, you can transform coincidence into destiny. Cadrenal went public because we were ready to go public onto Nasdaq when the window opened! You become the driver of your life, not just a rider.

As different as these circumstances were, several principles have been consistently helpful:

CONTROL WHAT YOU CAN CONTROL

Most people focus on what they can't control. They complain about the economy, or politicians, or how they're unappreciated at work.

CHAPTER 2: **THE COINCIDENCE OF DESTINY**

They expend all their energy on variables they cannot influence instead of channeling their energy to what they can influence:

- Attitude (e.g., gratitude, positive thinking, kindness)
- Efforts (e.g., work ethic, continuous learning, looking for opportunities)
- Vision (e.g., defining success for yourself, envisioning the destiny and life you want)

Instead of focusing on your dreams, focus on your vision. Some people see those as the same, but they're not. Dreaming isn't actionable—vision is.

As a kid, I dreamed of being a pilot like my dad. That dream evaporated after we left Vietnam. It had no room in my life when I was adapting and adopting. But then I went to an air show and saw the Blue Angels rocket overhead. My dream didn't resurrect. My vision ignited. I could envision myself in the cockpit, which stoked a fire in me. That fire set in motion the efforts that led me to the Marine Corps.

When I left the Marines for pharmaceutical sales, I envisioned myself as the top salesperson, despite the internal competition from established salespeople who said I'd never make it. That vision carried me to the top of the charts within a few years.

And when I left biotech sales to start up my first company—despite having no experience as a CEO—I envisioned winning a pitch competition as the quickest way to get funded besides using my own money. (I wholeheartedly believe you should have skin in the game.) And even though my number-two hire thought we would be lucky to get even $50,000 from the competition, we ended up walking away with $5 million in 2000. *Shark Tank* winners get a fraction of this!

Now, let's not look at this through rose-colored glasses. Not everything you envision will come true right away—or exactly how you expect. I envisioned being in the cockpit of a jet like a Vietnamese Maverick. Instead, I was given an assignment as a helicopter pilot. One of my previous startups ended up having to close up shop despite the success I had envisioned.

But the alternative is no vision. No vision. No effort. No results. It's an alternative many people choose because they prefer to settle and complain rather than try and fail. That's not the way of the underdog. The way of the underdog is recognizing that you can fail forward. Even when you're being tackled, you can still gain a yard or two. You control what you can control by adjusting your efforts to the results.

So much of the time, failure reveals that you either weren't in the right place, it wasn't the right time, or both.

PUT YOURSELF IN THE RIGHT ENVIRONMENT

You've heard it said that luck is being in the right place at the right time. Most consider luck as pure coincidence. But if you put in the effort to define even one of those factors, then you can transform coincidence into destiny.

Knowing the right time is next to impossible. But knowing the right place? That's a factor where you have some control.

You have to put yourself in the seat where you want to be. You can't do that until you learn as much as you can about where you want to be. For instance, if you envision yourself in your boss's job one day, then what are the actions you need to take now to prepare yourself? You can't count on them naming their successor and choosing you. Therefore, what are the efforts that will help you be ready for the role from day one? You have the ability to start now.

CHAPTER 2: **THE COINCIDENCE OF DESTINY**

It could be as simple as reading a book, taking a class, or earning a new certification. For me, it was persuasive public speaking. If you envision a different role in a different department, it could look like going to that department head and asking to shadow their staff for a day.

But let's say you lack fulfillment with where you are right now. That should be a major red flag. You need to ask yourself why you're still there. Is it a lack of vision because you haven't defined your own success? Or are you being held back by the fear of making a change?

No doubt about it—change is uncomfortable. It forces you to accept that you've possibly spent too much time in the wrong place. Change forces you to adapt. But the longer you put off being in the right place, the more likely you are to lose your shot at the right time.

When I chose to leave the Marine Corps, it would have been easy to fall victim to the sunk cost effect—to feel like I had wasted my time and all those flight hours that could have landed me with an airline. But when you see coincidences as part of destiny, then there is no such thing as wasted time. The first investor I ever secured for my first startup was someone who could appreciate my military background—Naval Academy graduate and aviator Dan Beldy. His partner's father was also a Marine who had served in Korea. I went two for two with investors. Coincidence or destiny?

Once again, you must start with the end in mind—success. You have to be able to see where the right place is for you. Only then can you start taking the right efforts at the right time. Only then will so-called luck come along to help you transform all your coincidences into destiny. I had visualized myself in winning situations in *all* my endeavors.

BE AROUND THE RIGHT PEOPLE

You can't be in the right environment without also being around the right people. If you're looking around and don't see any of the right people, then you're likely in the wrong environment.

Being around the right people involves some effort on your part. You have to seek them out. In terms of professional networking, successful people don't network just for the sake of networking. They have a target in mind. They've identified *who* they want to network with and zero in.

But knowing who the right people are is only half the battle. The other half is finding the common ground you share with them, then convincing them to invest in, partner with, or support you.

Not long after I was hired by Astra/Merck for my first pharmaceutical sales job, they held a national sales meeting. At the VIP reception, the six-foot-five CEO walked in—Wayne Yetter. I was still in my first three months, but I'd done my homework on Wayne and learned he was a Vietnam vet. So I walked up and introduced myself.

My colleagues—even the more seasoned ones—couldn't believe I'd had the guts to walk up to him like that. But why wouldn't I? I knew Wayne was a people person and we had Vietnam and military service in common. I was able to thank him for his service and share about how my dad had fought alongside Americans.

Wayne was exactly the type of person I needed to be around, learn from, and grow with. Later on, he was a director for my first startup—MyDrugRep.com (Lathian Systems)—and also became *the* key board member for my second startup, Espero BioPharma. He's also been a fine golf buddy.

Was it a coincidence Wayne was there that day? Maybe. But my decision to be around him was destiny.

CHAPTER 2: **THE COINCIDENCE OF DESTINY**

Integration

Sports was the first arena where I learned to integrate all three of these concepts: controlling what I could control, being in the right environment, and being around the right people.

It started with common ground. In Vietnam, I was always running around, playing badminton and soccer. In the US, soccer wasn't as popular, but baseball was. Though the sports couldn't be more different, learning the game was something I could control. Not only would it allow me to develop more common ground, but it would help me better adopt my new environment by practicing my English more (and cursing).

Even though some of the parents were negative about my abilities—or rather, lack thereof—the kids took me in. They helped me make the transition from being an outsider to an insider by choosing to become part of a team, something bigger than myself—my first team in America, the Indians of Oxnard. (Although, my first professional team to root for was the Los Angeles Dodgers.)

It wasn't the obvious choice. After that first game when the wind got knocked out of me and everyone was laughing in my face. I was on the verge of tears, and it would have been easier to run home and never go back. But the underdog in me fought back. Now I had something to prove. And I knew the right place and right people to prove it to.

While natural talent is always a major component for any sport, it's not the only one. Practice is the other. And especially in baseball, you can improve your talent through practice. Once again, this was an area where I had some level of control. I could put in the hours both on and off the field to improve my fielding and batting skills.

Sports helped me realize that you only had to be better than average. In high school, I went from never playing organized basketball to become the starting point guard and team captain during my junior year. Basketball became my lifelong team sport, and running full court games at the local YMCA is still part of my routine, albeit at a much slower pace. I realized if you could be better than average, then you'd make it on to the field and the court in America. And down the road, into foursomes at country clubs where business deals are often made.

Fifty years ago, the sight of an Asian kid on a US baseball diamond was a novelty. I would have never imagined that two Asian men would be among the best players in the MLB today. Yet as I'm writing this, Shohei Ohtani boasts over fifty home runs, over fifty stolen bases, and a batting average of .310. And Yoshinobu Yamamoto is one of the best and highest paid pitchers in the world. Both belong to my team, the LA Dodgers, who won the 2024 World Series. And five-foot-eight, lightning-quick point guard Yuki Kawamura just made the roster of an NBA team.

It just goes to show that opportunities will come along if you put in the effort and results for the destination you want. But it will require some discomfort. It will require you to integrate yourself into the right environment around the right people.

Segregation is the option many choose because it's comfortable. It's what many of my fellow refugees chose, staying around people who looked like them, talked like them, and thought like them. But if you choose to integrate by finding that common ground with others who appear different from you, you double your opportunities. You increase your chances of transforming coincidences into destiny.

The secret to integration is that you need to be a little bit of an outsider *and* an insider. If you're already an outsider, then you have to accept the norms, expectations, and the creed of the society or organization you find yourself in. *Walk their walk.* That's the adoption piece coming into play. You can't make changes as an outsider. Only insiders can do that. Changes come within.

Yet you have to maintain enough of your outsider's perspective to see the challenges that need to be fixed. Otherwise, you will sink to the status quo. As an outsider-insider, you can set yourself apart—and know when to pivot. It's a hybrid position I have lived in for all my life.

Reflaction—The Pivot

Isaac Newton's third law of motion is one of the building blocks of physics. It simply states that "for every action, there is an equal and opposite reaction." For our purposes, you could tweak it to say, "For every effort, there is an equal and opposite result."

That's the art and science of the pivot. When you pivot on the basketball court, you're performing basic physics. To pivot *left*, you have to turn your right heel to the *right* while using your toes like a hinge.

Pivoting is a skill I've had to practice in every career—military, pharma sales, and entrepreneurship. Everyone needs to know how to pivot. Which is why I enjoy learning about the diamond-in-the-rough drugs in the market.

For instance, everyone knows what Viagra can do. And yet that's not at all what it was designed to do. It was initially developed to treat high blood pressure and angina (chest pain). But during the clinical trials, the drug showed different results. It was an unintended consequence—an opposite reaction from what the developers were working toward. And yet, it worked. The results reshaped their efforts. They pivoted and went on to release a drug that quickly became a household name. Same goes with Ozempic, the weight-loss blockbuster that began its life to treat diabetes.

Coincidences will continue to come your way, whether they are the result of others' actions or unintended consequences of your own actions. Either way, you'll have to pivot. It's all part of taking yourself to the ER.

Coincidences rarely come at convenient times. You'll likely be facing some form of restriction, whether it's time or resources, or a commitment to other priorities. An opportunity may come along that aligns with your envisioned destiny, and yet you may not have the bandwidth to take advantage of the moment.

So your reflection for this chapter is to consider where you need to pivot so you have the bandwidth to turn coincidences into destiny. Depending on where you are, ask yourself these *pivotal* questions:

- If you're facing an unexpected change, ask: "What do I need to do so I can adapt? What is actually in my control?"

- If you're not getting the results you want, ask: "Where do I want to be? What are the attitudes and behaviors I need to adopt?"

- If you are getting the results you want, but progress still feels slow, then ask yourself: "And then what? What can I be doing above and beyond? Who are the right people I need to be around?"

- If you feel stuck between two paths, ask: "What do I need to do now that I can't do later in life?"

Now, from those answers, take the following actions:

- Identify one habit you need to adopt this week to increase your efforts. Maybe it's waking up earlier to exercise or meditate. Maybe it's taking a half-hour lunch instead of an hour so you can fit in more sales calls.

- Identify one way you can move closer to the right environment. It could be attending a networking event, taking a training course, or reading a book.

- Identify one right person you need to get closer to. Perhaps it's a mentor, your significant other, or an old friend. Reach out and schedule a time to meet up.

Even if you don't get the results you hope for with each of these tasks, you'll at least become more adept at adapting and adopting. You'll gain more clarity around the destination you want. Piece by piece, you'll take the coincidences life has given you and use them to write your own destiny. They will line up one day for you, so be ready.

My father as a newly winged pilot by the US Air Force in 1959 (Author's Collection)

Me and my late father, my hero, after his return to the US (Author's Collection)

AVENUE OF APPROACH 1
COMMIT

CHAPTER 3

Love What You Do Until You Can Do What You Love

But the grass ain't always greener on the other side. It's green where you water it.
—JUSTIN BIEBER, "AS LONG AS YOU LOVE ME"

I wasn't always so decisive. As mentioned in the last chapter, this was a skill I didn't pick up until the Marines. Even though I can now look back and see the Marine Corps was part of my destiny, I almost didn't even join.

For about five months, I strung along the recruiter Doug Hamlin, saying I was still thinking it over. The summer training I went through to be a Marine was not only physically tough, but culturally and mentally tough. The Corps was not very diverse back then at all. I was one of the few Asian faces in a sea of white, along with a couple of Blacks and Hispanics.

The Marine Corps was the last service to integrate Blacks, last to allow women to fly, and had the lowest percentage of minority officers, especially among its generals. The television show *60 Minutes* even aired an exposé and interviewed several Black officers. In fact, the cultural barrier was the primary reason I initially decided not to move forward—but I kept that decision to myself as I went back to UCLA for my senior year.

Two defining moments pivoted me. The first was the Vietnam Veterans Memorial wall in Washington, DC, first dedicated in 1982. The week before graduating from Officer Candidates School (OCS), my friend Mark Henderson said he wanted to go see the wall. His dad had been a fighter pilot in Vietnam, and I said I would go along.

There I stood in front of that glossy black wall, covered with fifty-eight thousand names of men who had died in my country—and a realization hit me like a brick. Though I was a survivor of the war myself, I didn't know a single name on that wall. Despite all the mixed feelings about the Vietnam War, I had to ask myself, "What if America hadn't come to Vietnam? What if these men hadn't fought and died? What would my life be like? Would I be living under a Communist regime? Would I even be alive?"

It was an emotional moment that made me recognize I had my own personal Vietnam syndrome. I had an awakening to repay the debt to the US for taking in our family and giving us a new start.

Coupled with this was the knowledge that I had already passed the screening for OCS. And since no Vietnamese refugee had made it through both OCS and flight school, I definitely had the internal motivation to do what others said was impossible.

At war with these feelings was the knowledge that I needed a career. As my graduation from UCLA sped toward me, I needed money. So I had also been talking with recruiters from Dean Witter Reynolds and other companies about an entry position, thinking it might be the safest professional route for a new college grad.

CHAPTER 3: **LOVE WHAT YOU DO UNTIL YOU CAN DO WHAT YOU LOVE**

Then the second defining moment happened when I returned to school. The Marine recruiter, Captain Hamlin, drew a line in the sand, point blank:

"Q, when we first met, you told me you always wanted to be a Marine pilot. So what's actually holding you back?"

I didn't want to show all my cards—my Vietnam syndrome. So I simply answered, "I'm not sure I see the Marine Corps as a long-term career. I'm thinking about going to work as a financial analyst instead."

He nodded and then gave me some of the best advice I've ever received. "I understand. But consider this: Business jobs will always be there if you decide that's what you want to do. No one's asking you to sign up for twenty years in the Marines. But there's a cutoff age for becoming a military pilot. You have to finish pilot school before you turn twenty-nine years old. After that, it's not possible."

This FOMO-fueled proclamation was exactly the push I needed. He was right: business would always be there. The window for becoming a pilot was shrinking every day. Up until then, I'd been straddling the fence, one foot in and one foot out of the Marines. But I needed to jump in, both feet. I had to commit.

After flight school, I faced another dilemma, though. I had poured everything into training, given it my best efforts, and studied harder and flew better than my peers. I envisioned myself in that jet cockpit, following in my dad's footsteps and defending my adopted nation.

But here's the thing you might not know about military fighter/jet pilots—even if you qualify, a limited number of seats are available. Some of my buddies made it into jet pilot training right away—but I was left out. The needs of the Marine Corps always came first before your personal preference, so I was assigned to be a helicopter pilot. There were two pilots required to fly every helicopter, therefore, more seats.

This was my first professional disappointment in life. It felt unfair that I had met the requirements and yet was excluded. I even wrote a protest letter to our training CO about the injustice of the decision. Though, in retrospect, that wasn't the best idea since he himself had been a Navy helicopter pilot. His handwritten response was understandably terse:

"Request denied. The Marine Corps needs helicopter pilots. You'll have a great career. Good luck."

Frustrated, I went into helicopter training with less than full enthusiasm. It wasn't the destination I had envisioned. It wasn't my definition of success.

You might think you're good at masking your disappointment well, but I can assure you, there will always be someone who can sniff it out. For me, that guy was an older and cranky Marine pilot at my first duty station. He was married to a retired four-star general's daughter and exuded an air of being untouchable. And man, he did *not* like me at all. I remember him as Captain Jerk.

He could tell I didn't really want to be there and rode me hard, trying to wash me out. He screamed at me in the cockpit, calling me "Mongoloid" and "Phlegm Pham" among other offensive names. And then he wrote a report saying, "Q needs extra flight time" and put me on a remedial training program.

Once again, it was just the wake-up call I needed. Only then did I realize how closely I was being watched and that I wasn't bringing my best effort.

Instead of the remedial program, I was assigned to fly with an experienced Vietnam vet for my check ride. He was one of the many good guys in the Corps. Fair was fair. After three intense hours of flying the check ride, he dismissed Captain Jerk's report and said, "Get outta here. You're going to your combat squadron."

CHAPTER 3: **LOVE WHAT YOU DO UNTIL YOU CAN DO WHAT YOU LOVE**

Maybe you're reading this book because you feel stuck or jaded. Maybe you didn't get the promotion or assignment you wanted. Maybe you feel like you've been passed over a hundred times. The first action you have to take is to heighten your self-awareness. You need to be hyperaware of the attitude you're bringing to the table. Because it only takes one influential person to sniff out your disappointment and chalk it up to laziness. It could end your career the way it nearly ended mine.

Even when you don't get the results you wanted, you still have full control of your efforts after the disappointment. Will you let disappointment rule over you? Or will you reevaluate and recalculate the math?

For me, that meant taking a fresh look at the success I had defined for myself. I had defined it as being named a fighter/jet pilot because that's what I knew. That's what my dad had been—a propeller-driven fighter pilot, a Skyraider pilot, la crème de la crème. I hadn't considered that a helicopter pilot is still a pilot. Nor did it mean the door to becoming a jet pilot was closed forever. I had met the requirements, but no seats were open. If I didn't get my act together and give it my all, then a seat would never be open to me.

In hindsight, becoming a helicopter pilot was the best thing that could have happened because that's the only reason I had the chance to unleash my inner underdog and go defend another underdog nation. All my buddies who went to jet pilot training missed out on the Gulf War. Had I been assigned to jets right away, then I would have never fulfilled the vision I had set for myself.

I learned to love being a helicopter pilot, even though it wasn't my first pick. Helicopter aircrew is a team in the air, two pilots up front and up to four crewmen/corpsmen in the back. Plus a squad of grunts or infantry Marines who are our most precious cargo.

But it was my own responsibility to generate enthusiasm for the role. I learned a major lesson—you have to love what you do until you can do what you love.

Wherever you are now, you have to make the best of it. If you're always one foot in, one foot out, it's going to show in your effort and results. Right or wrong, you make a decision. You take yourself to the ER and pivot as needed. And you commit to excellence until you reach your jumping-off point.

The Jumping-Off Point

So far the advice here might sound like "white knuckle and bear it." But the reality is that if you define your destination first, your effort and results will lead you to the right jumping-off point. This isn't a blind jump into the abyss—it's a calculated jump where you know your target landing and have your parachute ready to go.

The danger of living one foot in, one foot out is that you're splitting your attention. You want to leave in search of greener pastures, but what are you going to do when you get there? Are you going to have the tools you need to keep the grass green?

Finding greener pastures will go much better for you if you're already watering the one you're in. If you find a way to love what you do now, then you develop the tools and resources you'll need later on for the so-called dream job.

One reason I don't like to refer to *dream jobs* is how the term sets up a false expectation that you can only be personally and professionally fulfilled once you land *and live* your dream job. Wherever you are now, develop a vision for success that allows you to love what you do rather than withhold your passion until the mythical dream job arrives. Especially if you need multiple jumping-off points to reach your destination.

For example, let's say you want to be an entrepreneur. If all you've ever known is working for a large company providing you a salary and benefits, then what are you doing to prepare? Do you have enough money saved up to go twelve months without pay and health benefits? Are you prepared to use up your savings to pay others? Or downsize your living situation?

If not, then it might make more sense to first join another startup rather than start your own. You'll still be taking a risk, but you won't be taking the biggest risk. At least then you'll be able to build up some experience with entrepreneurship but without assuming all the liability. You can be the "aide-de-camp" to the entrepreneur—close enough to see whether it truly matches your definition of success.

In the age of the side gig, it's easy to think you can be a weekend entrepreneur. If that's the path you're considering, I'll let you in on a little secret: No investor is going to give you money if you're not fully committed, all-in. And most of the time, you will need to have a lot of skin in the game—put in your own money first.

Even if you're looking to jump to a new company, this idea still holds true. Do you think anyone will want to hire you if you tell them you're going to keep working at your old job twenty hours a week? Of course not.

My last year in the Marine Corps confirmed what I had suspected since the beginning—it wasn't to be a long-term career. I loved the challenges, camaraderie, and professional skills I had acquired as an active duty officer, but I also knew that I had fulfilled my personal definition of success. I had achieved a peace of mind by overcoming my Vietnam syndrome. I had become a *real* American. No one could deny me that status. Now it was time to find the next challenge.

Being uncommitted to your present role has consequences. Yes, you're ready to leave in search of greener pastures, but you also have to keep tending the grass where you are now and leave it looking better than when you arrived. When I left active duty, I did so with an honorable discharge and high recommendations from my superiors that helped set me up for my next phase.

Another problem with having one foot in, one foot out is how it confuses your personal compass. You're looking too many directions at once. This conflict of focus doesn't promote mental wellness. But when you keep both feet firmly in, you are anchored—and you can better survey your options. And then, when you eventually make the leap, you can do so fully committed.

When approaching your jumping-off point, the worst action to take is to coast. Think about it like a long jumper in a track meet. Ever seen one slow down as they approach the take-off board? Of course not. They sustain their energy all the way through the jump for the best results.

Likewise, you have to approach your work with the same enthusiasm and energy that you did your first day on the job—even when you know your jumping-off point is approaching. It will save you from burning a bridge that you might need to cross later on.

The Marines did their best to keep me around. Some of my superiors alluded to seeing me become a colonel—or even general—based on my effort and results. This was clear when they saw me excel at the aide-de-camp assignment since those are roles typically assigned to more career-oriented officers.

During my last year on active duty, I kept my plans quiet. I knew I'd be going into the private sector, but I didn't know yet what the exact jumping-off point would look like. In a way, the mystery was a gift because it allowed me to keep giving a hundred percent, even as the clock was running out. The mission still needed to be completed, so I kept two feet in the present, with my eyes on the future.

Feet in the Present, Eyes on the Future

What if you don't have a jumping-off point determined yet? What should you do if you realize you're on the wrong track? How do you balance staying committed in the present while keeping an eye on the future?

This is the most difficult when you're miserable in your current job. Maybe you feel like you have no options, but you actually do. You always have the option to give your best by finding what you love.

Maybe you've heard of the 80/20 rule—that 80 percent of your results come from 20 percent of your efforts. There's a lot of truth to this idea, but it's most difficult to follow the 80/20 rule when you have no passion for where you are. You can't get the results without the effort. And it's difficult to force the effort when you are burned out.

If so, then turn the 80/20 rule on its head into the 20/80 rule. Find 20 percent of your job that you do like and give it all you've got. When you do, you'll get 80 percent of your results (or more) from that 20 percent.

Start identifying the skills you want to grow in. Even when you are making an industry or career shift, there are skills in every job that you can transfer over to the next role.

You need to feel like you're contributing to the success of the organization, even when you know it's not forever. Because the success you have there will be the building blocks for your destination.

As an aide-de-camp, I provided extensive administrative assistance to the general, which included many individuals in the business community. We were based out of El Toro in the middle of Orange County, California, so the general had many connections within the local business community—which meant they also became my connections.

Did I love being an aide-de-camp? No. I would've rather been back in the cockpit flying missions. But I found the 20 percent of the job I liked and gave it 100 percent.

The skills I developed in the role prepared me for the world of pharmaceutical sales. The decision-making matrix of "go/no-go" saved me from wasting time as a rep. I had to learn to be efficient with my time, stay on course, manage complex schedules, and communicate with a wide range of people. All while simultaneously building a network.

On the surface, the two jobs look unrelated, but the skills are totally transferable with the right approach. Remember in *The Karate Kid* how Mr. Miyagi trained Daniel? Daniel wanted to learn karate and grew increasingly frustrated that Mr. Miyagi had him waxing cars, painting fences, and sanding the deck. What Daniel only realized later was how Mr. Miyagi was developing his muscle memory through those seemingly unrelated tasks.

It's the same with the job you're in. You may not realize what muscle memories you're building up that you need in the next role—or the next.

When you make this 20/80 shift in your approach to be committed where you are, then it also makes you more valuable where you are. The opportunities you feel like you've missed out on may suddenly begin to open to you.

When I announced I would be leaving the Marines, my superiors doubled down their efforts to keep me around. That dream job of being a fighter jet pilot? Suddenly it was mine if I still wanted it. "Just say the word."

CHAPTER 3: **LOVE WHAT YOU DO UNTIL YOU CAN DO WHAT YOU LOVE**

It was a tempting offer, but the Marines had taught me to be decisive, not to waffle around. So I stuck to my plans and left active duty. But I did at least finagle a few supersonic flights in the backseat of a USMC F/A-18D Hornet!

Flying a fighter jet was no longer my definition for success. I had a new vision, an improved definition of success. But I never would have found it if I hadn't learned to love what I was doing. Staying committed prepared me not only for my first jumping-off point into pharmaceutical sales, but even laid the groundwork for jumping into my first startup.

Underdog Strategies for Success

Let's get practical with these philosophies now. The approach of the underdog will help you excel in your current role even as you prepare for future goals. Why? Because that's what underdogs do—they keep driving to the future even as they apply their effort to the present.

Several underdog strategies can help you love what you do until you can do what you love.

The first is time management. It's human nature to do the easiest tasks first, but underdogs fight that nature. They do the most important stuff first. When you prioritize the most important tasks, you're aligning your efforts to your results.

Sometimes the most important task will take the most time, which is why you'll be tempted to put it off. But you must fight that urge.

This applies in entrepreneurialism too. If you're delivering a pitch to a potential investor, don't save the most important slide for when you only have five minutes left. Lead with it. You may want to tell a story while investors want to hear the pitch.

59

The second strategy is to build a rationale around every task. Even when you don't see how the skill could possibly help you in the future, create a reason. You don't know the future, after all. Craft a story for yourself for why that skill will be needed later on. Think to yourself, *This is going to make a great anecdote one day for my book.* You never know!

The third strategy is to aim high. Always.

In high school, I took the hardest classes, tried out for basketball even though I had never played on a team, and went after the girls who were out of my league. No one was helping me out. It was all up to me. People thought I was either completely naive or had unbelievable confidence. Neither was true.

I had simply seen that when you aim high, even when you fail, you're further than where you started. The "no" you get today becomes fuel for tomorrow. There's no downside to approaching your work with enthusiasm. Literally none. Even when you don't get the result you want, people will appreciate your attitude. Even when those girls turned me down, I'm sure the attention gave them a confidence boost. People remember when you make them feel good. And those good feelings often come back around. Though I'm not here to kiss and tell how I outkicked my coverage.

Don't get down on rejections. See them as hurdles to overcome. When people jeer at you for aiming high, look for the ones who cheer. Find your supporters. Focus on the good around you by holding your head high. The detractors just feel threatened or jealous that they don't have the same gumption as you.

Writing my first book looked like a fool's errand. No one cared about refugee stories back then. The world was still reeling from 9/11, not talking about Vietnam. I wasn't world famous—and I'm not a war hero. Who would want to read it?

But two people believed in me: My late Vietnam vet, basketball buddy, Mike Tharp (who was also an esteemed journalist) and my literary agent, Flip Brophy. We received twenty-plus rejections, but she kept telling me to aim high. "We only need the one yes," she would say. And then we got the yes from Random House. That's what the underdog approach of aiming high can do.

When I joined the Marines, I was an underdog. When I left to work for Astra/Merck as a sales rep, I was an underdog once again. When I wrote my first book, I was an underdog. But if you can prioritize what's most important, create a rationale for what you're doing, and aim high, you will put in the right efforts to achieve the right results.

Give it a try. You have nothing to lose. Everything to gain.

Reflaction—The 20/80 Rule

You might be at a point in your career where you know that you're ready for more, but you don't know how to define *more*. Maybe you're now aware that you're one foot in, one foot out and that you're committing self-sabotage.

To break free, you need to follow the 20/80 rule—find the 20 percent of your job you love and thrive in. For this exercise, clear your schedule, turn off your phone, and pull out a pen and paper. Yes, go old school.

First, don't think about the stuff you don't like about your role. Only write down the parts of your job you enjoy. Even if it's something simple like "attending lunch and learns" or "bringing snacks for my coworkers." Those count!

Second, write down what you do better than any of your peers. This is easy if you're already a competitive type. If that's not you, keep in mind that no one is going to see the list you're writing. It's only for you. Are you better at getting reports in? Write it down. Better at making people laugh? Write it down. Better at asking questions? Write it down.

You've likely only been comparing yourself to your peers in terms of the success defined by your boss and organization. But when you define success on your own terms, you get to recognize your own metrics for *better*.

The 20/80 rule is all about doubling down on your strengths. When you become more focused on your strengths, so will others. Instead of being committed to a company or job title, you'll be committed to your vision of success.

Stop thinking the grass is only greener on the other side. Water the grass where you are. Love what you do until you can do what you love. When you do, you'll maximize your efforts, improve your results, and take individual accountability for your success.

CHAPTER 4

Individual Accountability

Có tât giât mình. He who excuses himself, accuses himself.
—*VIETNAMESE PROVERB FROM* **THE TALE OF KIEU**

The photograph of six Marines raising the US flag atop Mount Suribachi on the island of Iwo Jima instantly became one of the most iconic images of World War II. The photo, snapped by Joe Rosenthal, won a Pulitzer Prize and was later enshrined as the US Marine Corps War Memorial in Arlington, Virginia. The story of the Marines raising the flag was even made into a movie in 2006, *Flags of our Fathers,* directed by legendary filmmaker Clint Eastwood.

To this day, Iwo Jima is considered one of the most remarkable moments in Marine Corps history. All told, 6,800 Americans—Marines and US Navy—lost their lives in the battle, with another 26,000 wounded or missing.[6]

---

[6] Blake Stilwell, "6 Reasons Why the Battle of Iwo Jima Is So Important to Marines," Military.com, February 19, 2021, https://www.military.com/history/6-reasons-why-battle-of-iwo-jima-so-important-marines.html.

During the course of World War II, a total of eighty-one Medals of Honor were awarded to Marines. Twenty-two of those were awarded to Marines for actions taken during the Battle of Iwo Jima. While the military is big on the idea of teamwork, it's worth pointing out that medals like the Medal of Honor are not awarded for team effort, but to *individuals* who show great valor, above and beyond the call of duty at the risk of one's life.

Teamwork doesn't happen if the members of the team don't take individual accountability for their role within the team. There is a responsibility to do your best because if you don't, you're not only letting yourself down, but you're negatively impacting everyone else around you. Marines are never scared of our enemies, but more of letting our buddies down.

Now I have to touch on a detail I skipped over in the last chapter. Part of my reticence around joining the Marines was because of the anti-Asian sentiment I witnessed during the Marine summer training I had gone through. Films of Marines bayoneting Japanese and North Korean soldiers and flame-throwing Viet Congs were imprinted on my brain. Training scenarios based on Vietnam further pushed me to the edge.

Though a part of me still wanted to fulfill my childhood dream of being a military pilot, I also felt a strong sense of being unwelcome—still an outsider. When I was entertaining the job opportunity with Dean Witter Reynolds, I kept telling myself, "I proved I could make it in with my completion of OCS. That's enough. Time to go into the private sector."

Assimilation in America had also taught me how incredibly difficult it is to make changes from the outside. Hollywood had an oversized influence in how both the military and Asians were perceived. This was 1986—the same year that both *Top Gun* and *Platoon* came out, two very different films that made huge cultural impressions for the military.

With *Top Gun*, you had a movie that made military service look cool for the first time since the end of the draft. On the other end of the spectrum, you had the grittiness of Platoon, the first Vietnam film made by a Vietnam vet, Oliver Stone. And Francis Ford Coppola, a famous UCLA film school graduate, had already made *Apocalypse Now*.

Combine the likes of *Apocalypse Now*, *Platoon*, and *Full Metal Jacket* and you had a rather one-sided view of Vietnam—one that omitted the contributions of the South Vietnamese military. My dreams of being a military pilot had always been a more individual ambition, but I had to wonder if this opportunity was bigger than me.

A deep feeling of cultural responsibility grew inside. If I was to change the perceptions of Asians *in* the military, then I needed to be an Asian in the military. This feeling was then supercharged by the visit to the Vietnam Memorial with my friend Mark. I couldn't excuse myself without accusing myself. Keep in mind, I didn't know yet that I had been destined to be a Marine since before I was born.

So when the Marine recruiter Captain Hamlin told me they had officer training slots open and could guarantee me a place in flight school upon graduation, the childhood dream became a calling. Now there was emotion and accountability adding significance to my decision.

Individual accountability doesn't happen without emotion. You have to actually care about the outcome. When emotion is missing, then the work is an obligation, not a calling. Only when you have a sense of individual accountability can you take responsibility.

Taking Responsibility

Ever since 1883, the official motto of the US Marines has been *Semper Fidelis,* meaning "always faithful." It's a simple promise with significant meaning—a pledge of loyalty, honor, and commitment. It captures a sense of individual accountability to a larger community. The expression indicates you're taking responsibility—for yourself and for your fellow humans.

In chapter 1, I described the events of my first deployment to Kuwait. Even though I was the most junior member of the team, I had a responsibility to speak up when I noticed we were off target. Semper Fi.

Had I not said anything, several other scenarios could have played out. Perhaps one of the others would have noticed, spoken up, and then we would have course corrected. But we would have lost valuable time and possibly arrived at our target too late. In fact, two other helicopters ran out of fuel and were unable to continue their mission. When we arrived, we barely had any fuel left—so we could have also ended up stranded while lives were on the line.

If no one else had noticed, we could have flown right into enemy-occupied territory and taken fire. Instead of going in for a rescue, we could have found ourselves fighting for our own lives.

But once I spoke up and the others verified we were off course, we course corrected. We broke out of the smoky fields and spotted our target—Kuwait International Airport a few miles ahead with columns of Marine armored vehicles rolling in. We arrived on target and on time to pick up the wounded Marine and injured enemy combatants, then flew them to a battalion aid station in Saudi Arabia.

When you're lower on the corporate ladder, it's easy to think, *Someone else will take care of it. Someone with authority will see the problem.* But that's not necessarily the case. You may be given a list of responsibilities as part of your job function, but you can always choose to take personal responsibility for the well-being of the organization. And often that means speaking up, even when you're the junior person on the team.

Even when others have already noticed the problem you're pointing out, it's an opportunity to show that you are paying attention. It's a chance to show you're not afraid to speak up. Good leaders will appreciate your underlying sense of personal responsibility.

But let's say you don't have a good leader. Maybe you have the type of supervisor who feels threatened by your courage to speak up. Or maybe one who even condescends to you for "pointing out the obvious." Don't let someone else's insecurity become yours. Practice taking responsibility even when there is no immediate payoff for doing so. The muscle memory will serve you well.

Overcoming the Blame Game

In some ways, success and failure should be treated the same. If you take all the credit in success, then you should do the same with failure. The problem is that when failure happens, many people are prone to play the blame game. They scatter faster than the Iraqi military fleeing Kuwait.

Part of what I love about golf is that it forces you to take individual accountability. With a team sport, you can often blame others if you want—though blaming others isn't recommended if you care about good sportsmanship or team morale.

You don't get that option with golf. It's all on you. Your swing, your putt. Your score. Your effort. Your results. No matter what, you get full credit and full blame. I decided to be a closer and not a choker.

Overcoming the blame game is a personal choice. It starts by taking yourself to the ER—recognizing how your efforts created the results you see. But if you're blaming all the external factors at play, you're not looking at how you could have adjusted your efforts.

You can always find someone or something to blame. You can blame the weather, or the market, or an election. You can even blame the customers for not buying enough from you. But where is that going to get you? Nowhere. Blame keeps you looking backward.

The problem is when you're working somewhere that removes individual accountability. In such an environment, the blame game is easy to fall into.

When I was honorably discharged from the Marines in 1995, my first sales job was with Astra/Merck. Prilosec was positioned to become the next big blockbuster drug, and we used to joke that the medication sold itself.

At the time, the company organized us by clusters made up of six sales reps assigned to an area. Instead of having an individualized commission structure like most companies, our commission was based on the results of the cluster. And since we were in the LA cluster, it wasn't that difficult for us to hit our goal and earn the cluster bonus. At least, at first.

Prilosec had been a hot seller for us, but now a new drug had come out—Prevacid—and carved out some of the market share. Suddenly, our cluster found itself in an uncomfortable situation—we missed our goal. Then that quarter turned into another. In my second year with the company, our cluster didn't make our goal.

Suddenly, our cluster found itself in the middle of a blame game, pointing fingers at each other:

"Did you drop enough samples?!"

"How come you didn't pull your weight?!"

"Maybe if you'd followed up more ..."

When we realized blaming each other wasn't working, we found a new target—the company itself:

"Well, the company didn't give us enough of a marketing budget."

"They didn't prepare us for the competition from Prevacid."

But none of this addressed the real problem: we were focused on what we couldn't control instead of paying attention to what the results told us about our efforts.

In a sales role, you can't control who says yes to you, you can't control the competition, and you can't control the effort of anyone else on your team. But you can control how many sales calls *you* make, how many in-person visits *you* conduct, and how you allocate your own time and resources.

By shifting the bonus plan to the cluster's efforts, the company was trying to make us more accountable to one another. On paper, it sounds like a great way to create teamwork and minimize any toxic competitiveness. But the result was that if the team wasn't doing well, you lost motivation behind your own efforts.

In the throes of the blame game, I found myself thinking, *Why should I kill myself for everyone else? This isn't the Marines.*

Looking back, a better commission structure would have been based on 60 to 75 percent of individual efforts and 25 to 40 percent of the cluster's achievements. This type of approach would have emphasized individual accountability while still promoting collaboration. The best model is to have two layers of incentives: individual ("What's in it for me?") and big picture ("What's in it for others?").

To overcome the blame game, you need to transfer your emotions away from what you can't control and toward what you *can* control. Like it or not, much of your efforts are driven by your emotions. The more emotionally invested you are, the more individual accountability you will have.

And that's part of why Vietnam turned out the way it did. The US got caught in a blame game. Also, the US never had the same emotional investment as either the South or North Vietnamese did, therefore less accountability. No US general lost a star over Vietnam. No one got demoted. No one was held accountable for lives lost.

The way I see it, the US didn't lose the war in Vietnam because the US still exists. South Vietnam doesn't. No one in US leadership went to prison for the decisions made in Vietnam. But thousands of South Vietnamese did go to prison camps—my father included.

Please don't see this as an accusation or as a slight against Vietnam vets. They are heroes and individuals who had to take accountability for elements outside their control. And there's nothing to gain from blaming others.

Playing the blame game has major pitfalls. Throwing others under the bus is a short-term solution that leads to a long-term problem. You end up breaking trust and hurting your reputation. Plus, "snitches get stitches."

In the Marines, we briefed and debriefed before and after every training mission to look for where the errors were made. From preparation, to execution, to the return flight to base or ship, we spent hours debriefing because it forced us to each take accountability for how our individual efforts contributed to the results.

When I was in pharma sales, we also did a ton of prep work—role-playing sales situations, practicing objections and questions from physicians, learning the benefits, features, and side effects of different therapies. But we rarely debriefed, which is a missed opportunity for the private sector.

If you want to avoid the blame game, you've got to do the same. You have to get into the habit of debriefing every "mission" you go on. When the results are what you hoped for, take accountability by making a plan to repeat the success. When the results are not what you hoped for, take accountability for your failings so you can improve upon them.

One time I was asked whether there is ever an appropriate time to take one for the team. That is, should you take the blame even when a situation isn't purely your fault?

This largely depends on what stage of your career you're in and your level of tenure in the organization. Assuming you're in a management position of some kind, there may be times when the team is stuck and no one else is willing to take responsibility. In those situations, it's often appropriate to take responsibility yourself so the team can move on and grow.

But if you're not managing others or you are still very new to the organization, it's best to stick with individual accountability—control what you can control. Otherwise, it could cost you status, or you'll turn yourself into a target. You don't overcome the blame game by putting yourself at the center of it.

The Power of Failure and Rejection

When I was hiring for my first startup, the first wave of hires was solid—great people who were bought into the mission and had the necessary knowledge and experience. But when it came time for the second round of hires, I made a rookie mistake.

After studying the profiles of those who were working at other successful startups, I saw a pattern—they seemed to all be people with Ivy League credentials and Silicon Valley connections. Instead of doing my due diligence, I became fixated on prospects' credentials. If they had Stanford, Harvard, or Wharton for their pedigree, then that was all I needed to know.

When we blended the initial management team with this second wave, they didn't gel as quickly as expected. Within a year, the people in the wave of prestigious degrees had all departed. Some of the members had never fully integrated into the organization. Others had come in eager to take on additional assignments, but we simply weren't ready to dole out more responsibilities or promotions to satisfy them.

I had to take responsibility as a first-time CEO. After all, I was the one who had the plan, put in the first dollar, and pulled the team together. I had expected the second wave of hires to do well with on-the-job learning, but not everyone did. I had also assumed their contacts in the investment banking world would translate into investors, but none of them panned out.

Was it a mistake? Most certainly. That wave of hires had been costly because of their pedigrees. They had looked good on paper, and I had to learn the hard way that paper wasn't everything. And now the business plan was going to be disrupted while we replaced their roles.

It wasn't a situation that could be redeemed, and it set us back from where we needed to be. But by taking accountability for the mistake, I've been able to avoid making it again.

The power of failure is how it gives you the chance to make accidental discoveries. Failure helps transform coincidences into destiny.

The world of drug development is especially prone to failure. The failure rate for clinical trials is high. The risk to investors is high. But so are the potential benefits to patients. It's an industry where you have to become immune to both failure and rejection.

It all comes back to the ER approach—looking at your effort and results. When you have your clear definition of success, you can recalibrate your effort and results no matter how many failures or rejections you encounter. Like Jack Andraka did.

When Jack was only fifteen years old, he had an idea for a diagnostic test to detect pancreatic cancer better than the ones that had been developed by Big Pharma. He wrote up a proposal around his idea and started sending it to research labs.

His proposal was rejected 199 times. Some people would count this as failure, but not Jack. For him, he only needed one yes for success.

And on his next attempt, he got the yes he was looking for—from Johns Hopkins University, no less. According to author Brad Aronson, the resulting pancreatic cancer test is a hundred times more accurate than the competing tests—and twenty-six thousand times less expensive to produce.[7]

Plenty of other examples exist of people who failed on the way to success: Thomas Edison and his two thousand failed light bulbs, James Dyson and his five thousand failed vacuum cleaner prototypes. And there was Fred Smith of FedEx who had received a C on his business plan. None of these people were failures. They were underdogs.

Reflaction—Good FOMO

Sometimes the best cure for failure and rejection is a little fear of missing out, or FOMO. A moderate dose of paranoia around your job security can help you take the right amount of individual accountability.

The work environment has evolved. The old motto for work was "I did my job." If you met expectations, you could comfortably expect to keep your job and even get an annual raise. Not anymore.

---

[7] Brad Aronson, "Famous Failures: 23 Stories to Inspire You to Succeed," BradAronson.com, accessed October 21, 2024, https://www.bradaronson.com/famous-failures/.

Unless you're sitting in the boardroom, you don't know what constraints the company is facing—pressure from shareholders, regulatory changes, marketplace shifts. You have no control over any of those factors. You only have control over your own efforts. Therefore, you should assume you need to be doing the extra—doing more than what is expected. You need to be taking on assignments without expecting incremental pay.

For instance, when customer relationship management software (CRM) started to be implemented in pharmaceutical sales, some reps complained about needing to learn a new system when their old system for tracking leads worked fine for them. I chose to dive in and figure out how the CRM could make me more efficient. Within a year, I was the CRM expert for our district and asked to teach others.

On my own accord, I signed up for Toastmasters to improve my persuasive presentation skills. Then I was asked to give a presentation to a packed room of nonsales employees. Little did I know a group of company VPs would be sitting in the back, listening to the presentation. Hours later, they were offering me to take over as the national sales trainer. All because of a little FOMO.

Good FOMO leads to constant learning. It's asking yourself, "What am I missing out on? What knowledge is out there that will make me successful?"

Most people are looking for effort and recognition, not effort and results. Recognition is a genuine human need, but if you are willing to delay recognition in exchange for results, then you will expedite your journey to success. Sometimes recognition and results go hand in hand. Sometimes they don't.

Results come from meeting or exceeding your goals. Recognition is when someone calls you out for doing the extra.

In the military, recognition happens through medals. In sales, it happens through cash, rewards, trips, and sometimes promotions. If you're not getting the recognition you feel you deserve, leverage some good FOMO to ask what you're missing out on:

- "Are my results average or above average?"
- "Am I making an incremental difference?"
- "Is there a void in my career I need to fill?"
- "What is the extra I could be doing?"

Another way to leverage good FOMO is to ask if you are experiencing fulfillment. Fulfillment is a higher state of achievement. Fulfillment is about self-acknowledgement—feeling enlightened about the work you're doing regardless of the rewards and recognition. This comes down to a personal level—your individual accountability and self-recognition.

If you're waiting for someone to hand you satisfaction, you'll wait forever. You have to be honest with yourself, which may be the most difficult form of honesty.

Earlier in this chapter, I introduced the concept of doing "the extra," but now is the time to actually define what that looks like. Then apply the extra to the other three questions:

- How will doing the extra get you above-average results?
- How will the extra make an incremental difference?
- How will the extra fill a void in your career?

If you're unsatisfied in your role, see it as an invitation to do more. Don't wait for someone to ask you to do more—go look for the extra value you can add.

Some might say, "But then I'm doing more work for the same pay. Won't I be taken advantage of?"

It's possible. But you're not actually doing the extra for them—you're doing it for yourself. You're doing it so you can add to your experience, so you can find more to love about what you're doing now. And when you do the extra, you'll eventually find the person willing to pay you for it. Or you'll discover the extra is something you can build your own business around.

In the Marine Corps, I was always looking for the extra. In the private sector, I was always looking for the extra. When you do the extra, you go from ordinary to extraordinary. Stop waiting for people to commit to you and start committing to your own success.

When you use your good FOMO for constant learning, then you're taking more accountability for your efforts. By consistently taking yourself to the ER, you're focusing on controlling what you can control. You're harnessing your inner underdog, committed to your vision of success. Because once you're fully committed, you'll be ready to confront the obstacles that come your way.

CHAPTER 5

Be Ready When Your Number Is Called

Things turn out best for the people who make the best of the way things turn out.
—COACH JOHN WOODEN, UCLA MEN'S BASKETBALL
COACH OF TEN NATIONAL CHAMPIONSHIPS

One of the great underdog stories of all time is that of the 1980 "Miracle on Ice" Olympic hockey team who bested the Soviet Union—a team who had gone undefeated in the Olympic Games since 1968.

Meanwhile, the US team was made up of nothing but college kids who were used to playing *against* each other, not with each other. The US team had finished fifth in the previous Winter Games, and the 1980 team came into the Olympic Games seeded seventh. Winning gold was a pipe dream.

Coach Herb Brooks's goal for the team was simple—he wanted the US to be the best-conditioned team on the ice. This belief is reflected in two of his most famous quotes:

- "Success is won by those who believe in winning and then prepare for that moment. Many want to win, but how many prepare? That is the big difference."

- "Great moments are born from great opportunities."

You can't say it better than that. When you prepare, great opportunities and great moments follow. None of us can control the timing of the opportunity, but we can control the preparation piece of the equation through our efforts.

So the real question we all must answer is "Will you be ready when your number is called?"

After several years in pharma sales, I joined Genentech, the top biotech company in the world. All these years later, I have nothing but gratitude for the time I spent at Astra/Merck because they took a chance on a Marine pilot with no business experience and taught me the ropes of pharma sales. No doubt I wouldn't be where I am today without them giving me my first private sector job.

At Genentech, I was able to zero in on my effort and results through more individual accountability with my sales, which resulted in huge annual bonuses, plus awards and trips. My results didn't have to be tied to those of any other reps, which allowed me to begin honing my entrepreneurial skills. But also, I was drawn to the innovative work happening there. We were promoting new monoclonal antibody therapies (Rituxan and Herceptin) that could effectively target cancer cells—and my father was about to battle cancer at the time.

In the last chapter, I mentioned how I became the CRM expert for our sales district, but I was also taking Toastmasters to work on my presentation skills. On top of this, I had also received approval from Genentech to pay for my executive MBA program. I was doing the extra while also flying choppers on the weekends in the Marine Corps Reserves with my buddies.

Eventually, doing the extra was noticed. My regional manager approached me and asked if I would be willing to speak about the benefits of our breakthrough therapies to all the internal employees who were not front-facing salespeople—the marketing people and even a crew from the science division. At that time, I was the top sales rep in the bio-oncology division of the company.

"They want to better understand the perspective of the sales rep," he said. "That way there can be more consistency in how we think about our messaging, from development to market."

Since this was my first opportunity to incorporate some of my Toastmasters learning, I jumped at the chance. I worked on the presentation whenever possible, making sure I was entertaining, not just informational. Eventually, I had crafted a full-fledged thirty-five-to-forty-minute talk.

And once again, coincidences came together into destiny. Little did I know that two of the company's senior vice presidents had decided to attend the talk, watching from the back of the room. Next thing I knew, my manager called me to say, "Q, they want you to come in to be the sales trainer."

It sounds like an overnight success story, but it wasn't. It took months to become skilled at the CRM before I gained a reputation as the go-to guy. I was working overtime to get in my MBA studies and Toastmasters training. When the opportunity arrived, I was able to seize the day because I had done the extra to ensure I would be prepared.

Yet accepting the job offer wasn't as easy a decision as it might sound. See, by this time, I was already drafting my business plan for my first startup. Amid the height of the dot-com boom, I had a case of good FOMO and had already mapped out a timeline to leave

Genentech the following year. So even though they didn't know this, I knew the role was going to be temporary no matter what.

I didn't want to live one foot in, one foot out, though. If they felt I could add value to the company as a sales trainer, then why not take the opportunity? It was another skill that would help me as a budding entrepreneur. Keeping my eyes on the future while doing my best in the role helped me become more financially secure for the jumping-off point.

Underdogs don't really believe in luck. They believe in preparation. They recognize that if you put in the effort and adjust with your results, then you only need the patience to wait for your number to be called. Because who knows if it will ever be called again?

Power of Preparation

Many people believe they are prepared, but the question is whether they are preparing for the right stuff. The tail end of December 1999 saw hordes of people preparing for the biggest crisis that never happened—Y2K (Year 2000).

Grocery store shelves were emptied of canned goods and water. Doomsday zealots prophesied the end of the world. Arnold Schwarzenegger starred in a film titled *End of Days,* playing an ex-cop on a mission to stop the devil from getting married. It was a wild time.

The problem for many people is that they are indeed preparing and putting in the effort, but all for the wrong purposes. Or without any purpose at all. This leads only to burnout, frustration, and all too often, hopelessness.

But it doesn't have to be that way. Take yourself to the ER. The power of preparation comes full force when seen through the lens of effort *and* results.

CHAPTER 5: BE READY WHEN YOUR NUMBER IS CALLED

While everyone else prepared for Y2K, I was making preparations aligned to the success I had defined for myself. On January 3, 2000, I incorporated MyDrugRep.com the day after I resigned from Genentech. This was a meticulous mental process. Since Genentech was paying for my MBA, I had to make sure there were clean lines. Otherwise, there was a risk that anything I developed for MyDrugRep.com could be counted as Genentech's intellectual property.

"But Q, isn't that being one foot in, one foot out? Didn't you say *not* to do that?"

Correct. To be clear, I was not doing both at the same time. I was not doing pharmaceutical sales *and* running MyDrugRep.com simultaneously. Otherwise, it would have been even more difficult to keep the two separate. The prep work I was doing with incorporating MyDrugRep.com was me moving into the right lane, preparing to take the exit ramp.

The company and my colleagues were stunned that I was leaving, especially since I had just been asked to be the oncology sales trainer *and* I was on track to be the top salesperson of the year. Nobody was voluntarily leaving Genentech at the time since it was *the* top biotech company in the world with an incredible pipeline of products. Yet I needed to make my move, and I felt confident about how I was leaving. I transitioned my customers to reps who I knew would take great care of them and did my due diligence. That way, I could leave with no bridges burned and with sure footing.

In the time since leaving the Marine Corps, I had spoken to thousands of people, talking about Vietnam, sharing about my experiences in the Persian Gulf, and of course, presenting one-on-one pitches to doctors in sales meetings. With the Toastmasters training added to this, I was now prepared to take my presentation skills to the next level by pitching our startup to investors.

During my preparations, I had learned about a new venture capital firm that would be investing in early-stage internet-based companies called Hummer Winblad Venture Partners. They were going to host a massive global pitch competition—the largest of all time—in which the winner would be guaranteed funding up to $10 million.

The lead partner for the competition was Dan Beldy, who was a Naval Academy graduate and former F-18 pilot, so in the spirit of finding common ground, I knew we had shared military experience. Then there was John Hummer, a former NBA player who helped dub the competition "Nothing But Net," so I knew we had the common ground of basketball since it was the sport that I had played most and followed closely. And then there was Ann Winblad, whose father had been in the Marines, so we had all of that common ground.

I was convinced this couldn't be a coincidence. This was destiny!

The competition was to be run like the NCAA basketball tournament. To enter, you had to be either a student or faculty member of a university or business school. Since I was still in the executive MBA program at UC Irvine, this qualified us. But given this was such a low requirement, everyone and their mother applied. Competition would be fierce. Even our dean didn't believe we would be competitive.

All the participating startups were going to be put into a geography-based bracket and evaluated based on our business plans. A "Sweet Sixteen" would be picked, and then those teams would be flown to four different regions for a pitch competition. The four regional winners would then be the "Final Four" and flown to San Francisco for the final pitch to the venture capital (VC) partners themselves.

My second-in-command thought we were wasting our time with the competition. He felt we should be going out with our business plan through more traditional pitching routes. But my "go/no-go" brain had already decided—we were in it until the end. And I told

CHAPTER 5: BE READY WHEN YOUR NUMBER IS CALLED

him, "If we get to pitch in front of the partners in the finals, I know we're going to win."

Long story short, we made it to the Final Four and found ourselves at the swanky W Hotel in San Francisco, set to face off against the three other finalists—a team from Wharton, one from Berkeley, and one from London School of Economics. Harvard and Stanford didn't even make the final cut.

Even at this stage, my number two still thought we were wasting our time. He thought we would get $50,000 at most from the competition. After all, our assets were twenty PowerPoint slides and zero patents. In the final pitch, we would have thirty minutes to make our full business case.

My Toastmasters training kicked in. The presentation had to be human and entertaining. It was clear to me the partners were trying to make the experience fun with its March Madness–inspired setup. And yet all the other teams were far too formal.

Though I don't have any direct proof, I believe what put us over the top was the very last slide where we put a picture of a basketball going into the hoop. Printed on the side of the basketball was our actual banking information.

I said, "We're not just happy to be here. We're here to cut down the nets. So here's our banking information. Thank you very much."

The minute the slide went up, John Hummer started laughing and said, "This is great."

I knew then we had won. But it wasn't until later that night at the cocktail reception that we were declared the winner of $5 million. In less than six months, I had gone from being a biotech salesman to the CEO of a fully funded internet startup at the height of the dot-com boom. No contestant on the popular *Shark Tank* series has come close to winning a $5 million initial investment (for 33 percent ownership or $10 million pre-money valuation) of our twenty-PowerPoint-slide company. And that happened twenty-five years ago.

Take note—preparation isn't just about what you want to achieve. It's also about knowing what your audience wants to achieve. That final slide with the basketball hoop wouldn't have worked in any other setting. But it worked there because I had done my homework on who would be in the room and where to find the common ground. With the right information, you can put in the right efforts to achieve the right results.

You never know when your number is going to be called. So you better be ready for it. There's no time like the present.

Confidence

The difference between confidence and arrogance is whether you attract people—or repel them. So much of preparation is about developing confidence, not only in yourself but in others.

We won the pitch contest not only because I had learned to exude confidence on a stage but because the investors felt confident in the idea we had presented. When you show people that you know your message by heart, it develops trust and rapport. And that's not just true in entrepreneurship—it's true when you're pitching yourself for a new job that aligns with your definition of success. The more confident you are, the more convincing and human you will be.

The BSers aren't confident. That's why they have to resort to BSing. They have the external appearance of confidence, but it chips away easily.

When you're unprepared, it drains confidence from the decision-maker. It sends the wrong message. They might interpret your lack of preparation as, "Well, it doesn't seem like they really care so much

CHAPTER 5: **BE READY WHEN YOUR NUMBER IS CALLED**

about this job," or worse, "Why would I trust someone with this job when they can't come to the meeting ready?"

And they're not wrong to hold these assumptions. If you were in their shoes, you would feel the same way. Preparation is the first step in developing your professional reputation. Even if that job is a "no" or the investor is a "no," you can still leave a lasting impression. It may not be your last chance to pitch yourself to them. Or they might turn around and pitch you to someone else. When confidence and reputation collide, opportunities arise.

Confidence is key to both preparation and committing to your approach. You already know this if you've ever swung a golf club. If you waver at all in the swing, don't count on the ball going where you want it to. It's yet another aspect of golf I love—every time I pick up a club, it's a chance to practice confidence.

I like to live by the advice of Tiger Woods, who once said, "There's no sense in going to a tournament if you don't believe that you can win it."[8]

The wonderful thing about confidence is that you can build it at any time from wherever you are. You have the internet at your disposal to develop your credentials within your industry, network with the people you want in your circle, and develop your reputation.

Your reputation precedes you, building up confidence in others. You need to be aware of what is being written about you and take the effort to get yourself out there through podcasts, articles, and your own social media.

By the time I pitched MyDrugRep.com, there were already articles out there about me, from the Marines to Genentech. When

---

[8] Ben Smith, "The Best Tiger Woods Quotes: 'I May Be Outplayed, But I'll NEVER Be Outworked,'" GolfMagic.com, November 2, 2021, https://www.golfmagic.com/pga-tour/best-tiger-woods-quotes-i-may-be-outplayed-ill-never-be-outworked.

I was pitching my book proposal, there were articles about me that agents could find to see if I was the real deal. This created confidence in the publisher that I already had a platform—they could see my credibility through all the preparation I'd done.

Every so-called influencer out there started with zero followers. Every Fortune 500 company was a startup at one point, an idea that sprang out of a garage or a conversation between two people. You don't have to make it to have confidence, but you do need confidence to make it.

Confidence can be tough to build. I always had the unusual advantage of needing to prove myself, but that's not the case for everyone. So if you're not confident in your confidence yet, try the following strategies:

MAKE A DIFFERENCE WHERE IT COUNTS

Even seasoned marathoners can make the mistake of going out too fast, too hard in the first few miles of the race. When your adrenaline is going and the crowd is cheering, it's easy to take off faster than what you prepared for. The problem with this, of course, is that they don't give you a medal for finishing the first mile of the marathon but the last. Sixteen marathons have taught me this lesson well.

Making a difference where it counts goes back to prioritizing your time and your efforts. Anyone can do this. And the result is that it develops your confidence over time.

Whenever playing golf, I focus on playing the last three holes really well. This is the stage of the round when most people are wiped out. It's been a long day, they're tired of hauling around their clubs, and their mind is already back at the clubhouse. I know that if I take the approach of being committed to those last three holes, I'll automatically have more confidence and perform better. All because my mind is in the right place.

Likewise, this connects back to loving what you do until you can do what you love. If your mind is fixated on an elusive dream job, you won't have the energy to get there. Pour that energy into making a difference where you are, and it changes everything.

BE EARLY

Once again, this is a skill anyone can master. It takes no special talent to arrive early. Whether it's a work meeting, your kid's ballet recital, or an interview—show up early. You'll automatically feel more confident. Nothing saps your confidence more than being rushed.

When you plan to always be early, it forces you to prepare. You develop habits like putting your clothes out the night before, researching backup transportation in case a train breaks down, and having the time to grab your prospect's favorite coffee order so you can make a great first impression.

The earlier, the better. Give yourself the time to look over notes again, meditate, or pray. You don't want your nerves sabotaging the preparation you've already put in. Give the extra effort to be early and you'll gain incremental confidence with each rep.

ADOPT THE GO/NO-GO DECISION-MAKING MATRIX

This is the only skill on this list that requires some real practice. The corporate world thrives on risk management, forecasting, and analyzing a situation to death. And I do mean "to death" because often, by the time a decision is made, it's too late. You're either entering the market too late, or the market has moved on.

There is such a thing as overpreparation. This is what happens when you get stuck in the belief you're preparing but you never take action. It's a fool's errand—analysis by paralysis.

Anyone can benefit from the go/no-go decision-making matrix I learned in the Marine Corps. "Right or wrong, make a decision." You can always course correct if it's the wrong decision. But the more decisions you make, the better you become at making them. It's sitting on your hands, waffling around that will get you nowhere, debating the same thing over and over again.

The good news is that you can start practicing today. Everyday life is filled with opportunities to practice go/no-go decision-making. Whether it's deciding on where to go for dinner, picking a new profile picture, or asking someone on a date, you have a chance to develop your go/no-go sensibilities.

As you practice being more decisive, you'll also grow in confidence. And others will notice your decisiveness, further developing your reputation.

The caveat here is that there are also times for patience. When making a go/no-go decision, you have to ask whether you have all the information available and know what the expiration date is for the decision. In the Marines, it was life or death, so the window for decision-making was narrow. But with lower-risk situations like deciding on a movie to go see, the window is much wider, and you have more time to gather the intel you need, such as the following: How long is the movie? Did it get good reviews? Does it star an actor I like?

Not every decision is life or death. Keeping this in mind, you can make sure the window for your go/no-go decision is an appropriate size.

CHAPTER 5: **BE READY WHEN YOUR NUMBER IS CALLED**

Reflaction—Patient Preparation

To go a little deeper on the idea of patience, it can often be difficult to strike a balance between patience and readiness. You have to think like a goalie in soccer or hockey. There may be large sections of time where the ball or puck is farther away from you, the action at the other end of the arena. But that doesn't mean you get to slack off. The greatest goalies are masters of balancing patience and preparation.

Recognize that not everyone you bring into your circle has the same concept of time. When I'm interacting with individuals from Big Pharma, they are used to longer timelines and bigger budgets. These expectations change the conversation. But if I'm meeting with a VC investor or board member, they want a lean budget and fast results for shareholders.

In either situation, you can find balance by turning your own efforts to control what you can control.

At the same time, remember that time keeps moving, and the longer you wait to make a decision, the further ahead your competition is getting. The time is now. Tomorrow is today. And the longer you wait to prepare, the more opportunities you are giving up. Deals get stale like fish.

You can still give a hundred percent of your efforts to what you're doing now while preparing yourself for your next role. Ask yourself, "Can I do my boss's job?" If not, go acquire those skills. Whatever your boss is doing will still make you more effective—and confident—in your present station.

Then ask yourself, "Can I lead my peers?" If not, then read a leadership book, find a mentor, or attend a course. The better you learn to lead yourself, the more prepared you will be to lead others. And you'll compound your present efforts, making yourself more valuable to the organization.

Commit to practicing the three confidence-building skills:

- Make a difference where it counts.
- Be early.
- Use go/no-go decision-making.

You won't do them perfectly right away. But the goal isn't perfection—it's preparation. With more preparation, you'll gain confidence. With greater confidence, you'll be ready when your number is called. And when opportunity and preparation finally meet, you'll find the success you've committed yourself to.

AVENUE OF APPROACH 2

CONFRONT

CHAPTER 6

Identifying Barriers

Complacency breeds failure. Only the paranoid survive.
—ANDY GROVE, FOUNDER OF INTEL CORPORATION

Sometimes you don't know what's still buried inside you until it's dredged up to the surface by someone else. That's what happened to me on my first day at OCS in 1986 when I faced the most difficult emotional obstacle I ever encountered.

Once I committed to the Marine Corps, my patriotism shot through the roof. The doubts I'd had about the anti-Asian sentiment disappeared, and I was seeing the world through stars and stripes. This was my chance to prove myself to the world—to go prove myself as a young and new American ready to serve his country, just like the guys I'd seen in the old World War II movies.

From the airport, I climbed onto the yellow school bus to head to Quantico, Virginia, and as soon as we arrived, the sergeants started drilling us.

"Get off the bus, get off the bus!" they shouted. "Get on the f*cking line!"

So we hurried off and lined up outside as they read off our names. A large Black sergeant with a thick Southern drawl stood in front of me. His first words to me were, "Phang, Phong, Phan, whatever your f*cking name is, what are you doing here in my Marine Corps? Are you a Viet Cong spy?!"

Those words set me back about eleven years. Suddenly, I felt like a little refugee boy again—a foreigner, an outsider, a nobody. His words were the most shocking thing I'd ever had somebody say to me—totally unexpected.

In retrospect, our recruiter did his best job to prepare us for the experience by *not* warning us what OCS would be like. He wanted us to be in shock. Because the biggest test for the military—and indeed, for many other organizations—is whether you can endure in a new environment. Do you have the mental toughness to withstand being denigrated? Can you lead Marines in combat?

To this day, I don't know where my next words came from. After all, English was my third language—and in a moment of emotional stress like that, you tend to resort to your native language. But somehow, all I could think to say in response was, "I'm an American, sir. We were on the American side!"

Apparently that did the trick, though, because he didn't continue to hound me after that. And I'm glad for it because the moment was so wholly unanticipated that my eyes welled up with tears, and I nearly broke down and cried. I was totally unprepared for the moment.

Here it was, not even the first full day, and it set the tone for the rest of the summer. After eleven years, I still had this emotional barrier within me, saying, "You're not from here. Fifty-eight thousand American lives were sacrificed, and you lost your country anyway. Do you really think you have what it takes to be one of us—the few, the proud, the Marines?"

It was their job, though. They weren't there to be our buddies or camp counselors. They were there to shake us up. And I wasn't the only one they spoke to like that. They also shook up the Jewish kid from Dartmouth and the Black kid from South Carolina who was slow to speak. They shook up the Mexican kid from Texas. They were zeroed in on picking apart our weaknesses.

The pull-ups, running, shooting, flying—those weren't the toughest barriers I had to overcome. Running the Stone Canyon hills of Bel-Air behind the UCLA campus and all my time in sports had prepared me to navigate the physical obstacles. But I wouldn't be able to do any of those if I couldn't overcome this emotional and mental barrier within me.

If you can't get over those emotional and mental barriers, then how can you make decisions while you're under physical duress? Even for amateurs, you have to know you can make it the last 6.2 miles of the marathon. That you have the legs to get the important rebound and hit the free throws with the YMCA league championship on the line. That you can make a twelve-foot putt in front of friends and family to win a club tournament. That you can execute in the area of action when it really counts, when lives are on the line.

Everyone's emotional barriers look different. And it's human nature to bury them, to want to hide your cards from the world. But you can't play the game if you're not willing to put the cards down in front of people.

Imposter Syndrome

That first day brought my own personal Vietnam syndrome back up to the surface, and I nearly lost all the confidence I had gained since coming to the US—over a decade of assimilation almost down the drain from two sentences questioning my presence, going from officer contender to a foreign pretender.

Everyone is talking about the dangers of imposter syndrome these days—and for good reason. Whenever you're doing something new, or you're taking the road less traveled, the loudest people in the stands are usually the hecklers. But what do you do when the heckler is in your own mind?

That's what happened to me when I took my first pharma sales job with Astra/Merck. I had zero sales experience, and yet they assigned me to the LA territory—one of the largest in the country. I wasn't the only rep there, of course. Not only would there be external competition from other companies, but within Astra/Merck, I'd be competing against more seasoned salespeople with five to ten years more experience.

My internal heckler started saying, "What do you think you're doing?! How do you think you're going to make up for all the time they have ahead of you?"

Fair questions. In terms of my career, I was starting over.

Whenever the imposter syndrome crept in, I learned to step back and remind myself of all I'd accomplished in the military. If I could fly into an active combat zone, I could certainly walk into a doctor's office and handle a difficult receptionist. I also reminded myself, "They hired me and placed me in this territory, which means they think I'm just as good as the more experienced reps."

I pivoted back to what I could control. I hit the books to learn everything I could about our drugs and the science behind the medicine. I wanted to know more than the doctors. After all, they were plenty smart enough to read the information on a box if they wanted—what could I tell them that they couldn't learn anywhere else?

CHAPTER 6: **IDENTIFYING BARRIERS**

Astra/Merck was big on doing role-play as part of our ongoing training, so whenever the trainer asked for volunteers for a role-play exercise, my hand was always the first up. I wasn't afraid of public speaking anymore, and I knew I could only improve by getting more reps in.

By focusing on the factors you control, you won't silence imposter syndrome, but you can turn it on its head. You can transform it into fuel for learning. Most people treat imposter syndrome as a barrier. Underdogs treat it as a challenge—and then they rise to that challenge.

Also, most people are trying to get rid of imposter syndrome. They're trying to hit the delete key, to make it disappear altogether. But you can't. Once you accept it's there to stay, you can form a new relationship with it. It no longer has to be a barrier—it can become a building block.

Emotional Intelligence

Imposter syndrome is largely a mental challenge, but it would be disingenuous to ignore the emotional factor. Emotions are a driving force in our behaviors—and our behavioral responses play a prominent role in our efforts.

No denying it—humans are emotional beings. Failing to address this fact is a major oversight in your path to success. The greatest barrier you face probably won't be external—it will be internal.

I once had a boss who liked to say, "I don't want your feelings, just the facts." Needless to say, he was neither well liked nor respected. He was only worried about numbers and facts, with no concern for people's lives or problems.

He was the type who only hired people with few options. He was the founder of the company, an immigrant, and only hired other immigrants. So why did I even go to work for him?

Initially, he had brought me in by saying I could take over the company in three years. Since becoming a CEO was my definition of success, it appeared like the plan was aligned with my goals. But I quickly learned the succession plan was a false representation.

Once I had taken the job, the pitch changed. He said, "Well, when I step down, you can run the company until my kids can take over."

But these results were not aligned with my definition of success. I was forced to recalculate the math. Was I willing to put in another two-plus years working for him, knowing there was an expiration date on how long I was allowed to run the company?

On top of this, I saw how he spoke to the other employees. He never wanted to be questioned—employees were there to obey orders, to adopt his ideas—not have ideas of their own. I came to understand that part of why he had hired me was because he expected, with my military background, that I would go along with this militaristic style of leadership. And because the company had government contracts, he knew I'd look good in front of his contacts from the government.

Though I was being paid well, I didn't want to be a mascot or a pinch-hitting CEO. The math didn't add up to the equation of success I was working toward. Emotionally, it wasn't the place where I needed to be, so I left. And in leaving, left a lot of money on the table. That company was sold for $350 million two years later, and 5 percent would have been for my shares. But I never looked back.

Were my six months of effort there wasted? Of course not. Sometimes having an ineffective leader is the best way to learn what kind of leader *you* want to be. I learned that whenever I did run a company, I wanted to make sure human emotions were a priority.

Every situation is a chance to grow your emotional intelligence (EQ). You get passed over for a promotion—you grow your EQ. Your boss belittles you—you grow your EQ. A deal you thought was a sure thing falls through—you grow your EQ. With each emotional obstacle you confront, you turn losses into gains.

Whenever possible, you use your emotions to course correct. Sometimes that will mean standing up for yourself and your values. Sometimes it will mean leaving a job that isn't meant for you.

The most difficult barrier is when you're in a situation with no obvious course correction to take. This could include being let go from a job—maybe even your dream job. What do you do when you're left holding a bag of emotions with no place to go?

That's when you'll have to do the most difficult task of all—facing your emotional triggers.

Emotional Triggers

Whenever the drill sergeant called my loyalty into question, it was an emotional trigger for me. It reignited old feelings because I wasn't emotionally prepared for the challenge.

There wasn't much of a course correction to make either. I was committed to the Marine Corps now. Could I have quit? Sure. But quitting would have meant allowing the emotional trigger to win. It would have meant walking away from the success I had defined for myself.

As difficult as the moment was, I'm grateful for it now. It was the gift I didn't know I needed—confronting my trigger head on, processing the emotion, and then rising above it.

Unresolved personal issues will become triggers, and they can be set off in the most unexpected ways. This came up again in my first few years in pharma sales. When my internal heckler wasn't bothering me, other reps were happy to take its place.

Several times I found myself challenged by more experienced reps about my experience and what made me think I could handle the front lines of pharma sales. Never mind the fact none of these people had been in an *actual* frontline situation.

Whenever challenged, I'd often become defensive and resort to discussing my Marine experience. One time, the challenging rep laughed and said, "Well, then why'd you leave if you were so great at it? I think you'd be better off going back in."

Those words were another emotional trigger for me. In leaving the Marines, I had experienced a loss of identity. Perhaps not as dramatic as losing my country, but it was still a loss. Those first couple years out of the Marines were tougher than I let on—I felt displaced again in the civilian world.

The emotional trigger took me back to a "grass is greener" mentality. What if he was right? What if I had made a mistake leaving the Marine Corps? Had I thrown away the most important part of my identity? And for what? To be a drug pusher?

Your sense of self helps you make transitions in life—it anchors you. But when your identity is closely linked to a single role, then it's easy to lose that sense of self along with the role.

What brought me back from the conversation was a simple realization: My job wasn't to sell to other reps. My job was to sell to customers.

And guess what? The customers always liked me, citing my professionalism and responsiveness. There were doctors who would see me even though they never agreed to see other reps.

The emotional trigger elicited from my rival's words made me realize that I was only being challenged *because* they saw the progress

I was making. With this new understanding, my confidence was bolstered, not abandoned.

To deal with your own emotional triggers, you have to be highly cognizant of your past identities. This is true in any field, whether you're a military veteran entering the private sector, a teacher transitioning into owning a business, or a professional athlete leaving the game. Those past identities are part of your story and your glory, but if you don't become aware of the emotional triggers attached to them, they will hold you back from the new identity you need to form.

I'll always be a refugee. I'll always be a Marine. I'll always be a salesman. I'll always be a father, a son, a brother, and a friend. I am now a Floridian who spent much of my life in California, on opposing coasts. Those parts of my identity are never erased—but they haven't prevented me from building new identities aligned with the definition of success I was zeroed in on.

Possibly the toughest part about emotional triggers is identifying them ahead of time. They usually show up in the moment when you're not prepared for them, destroying your confidence.

But as much as is humanly possible, take the time to identify your emotional triggers. Think back to the times when you experienced fight, flight, or freeze. What happened? What are the trends? By revisiting those moments from a safe distance, you can gain some perspective and be better prepared for the next time they come around.

Your triggers are where your external barriers meet your internal barriers. You have to confront them. If you don't, you'll have emotional instability instead of emotional intelligence.

The Threat of Complacency

The greatest barrier facing any of us doesn't look like a barrier. *Complacency.* And the greatest danger with complacency is that it can reverse success.

Andy Grove, the late founder of Intel, was known for his paranoia about Intel going out of business, even when nearly every computer on the market had Intel technology installed in it. But Grove did something remarkable by reframing paranoia as a positive.

Even his book was titled *Only the Paranoid Survive.* His argument was that paranoia saves you from complacency. When you fight complacency, then you stay more alert to the threats around you—internal and external.

Another quote from his book says, "Complacency often afflicts precisely those who have been the most successful."[9] And he's not wrong. If you look at the famous case studies of the giants who have fallen in the past twenty years—Sears, Blockbuster, General Motors—you can see a recurring theme: they all became complacent with their success.

Complacency skews your efforts. It tells you that you're already doing enough. It tells you that you don't need to do the extra. Complacency tells you that you don't need to learn anything new.

And on all counts, it's wrong. Complacency will undo all your effort and results. It will pull you into self-sabotage mode and make you vulnerable to both internal and external threats.

If you've ever watched a military- or law-enforcement-based movie or show, you've probably heard someone say "Check your six." For pilots, the phrase "Check your six" refers to the need to be aware of any enemy pilot closing in from behind. Simply put, be aware of

---

9   Andrew Grove, *Only the Paranoid Survive (Crown Currency, 1999).*

your surroundings. Have a healthy dose of paranoia about the threats that could show up at any point.

Checking your six includes identifying your emotional triggers. It can mean keeping a tab on what the market is doing and what your competitors are up to. It means having a plan B when you're briefing the mission because in your personal Eisenhower Matrix, there will always be unknown unknowns.

Complacency is closely related to the fear of success itself. This seems counterintuitive for driven individuals, but it's incredibly common and leads to self-sabotage. A red flag is when people downplay success by making comments like "I'm happy doing what I'm doing." These are the people who, deep down, are afraid to advance even when they desire advancement.

Or these are the people who believe they have gone as far as they can, so why try anymore? I used to see this in the Marine Corps. There was a class of Marines we would refer to as ROAD Scholars—meaning "Retired on Active Duty."

Often, ROAD Scholars are majors who have reached the seventeenth-year mark in their career. They know by this point they probably won't make lieutenant colonel, so they start coasting for the remainder of their career. Their complacency results in them being placed in admin roles or supply depots. And you'll never see them end up excelling in the private sector. They've lost too much of their early drive to complacency.

Blaming everyone else for the barriers is a victim mentality. Your ultimate enemy isn't a toxic boss, lack of opportunity, or competition. It's complacency. And no one can fight it for you. You alone have to confront it.

Reflaction—Give a Damn

With the ER approach, you already have tools that can help you fight complacency:

- Go/no-go decision-making
- Doing the extra
- Taking individual accountability
- Loving what you do until you can do what you love
- Constant learning so you can be prepared when your number is called

And then one more bit of plain-language advice to add to the list: *Just give a damn.* Ask yourself if you truly care about what you're doing or if you're only there for a paycheck. It's such a simple test that you can do every day. Some guys I know always say, "I'm here to have fun at this golf tournament." To which I retort, "Me too, and I have way more fun when I win."

If your answer is "I'm only here for the paycheck," then you need to pay attention. Take some individual accountability by asking, "What do I give a damn about?" Do some emotional exploration to find the answer. And stay away from people who always say, "Who cares?"

Assuming you're currently working for someone else, then you're not doing them any favors sticking around when your heart's not in it. And you're definitely not aligning your vision for success with your efforts. Everyone wins when you turn your effort and focus to figure out where your heart is.

Start by taking an EQ test. You can find a number of respected options:

CHAPTER 6: **IDENTIFYING BARRIERS**

- The EQ 360
- BlueEQ Self-Assessment
- Emotional Capital Report
- The Emotional Quotient Inventory (EQ-i)
- Mayer-Salovey-Caruso Emotional Intelligence Test (MSCEIT)
- Six Seconds Emotional Intelligence Assessment (SEI)

Just pick one. Simply figuring out where your EQ is will help you give a damn, fight complacency, and identify the efforts you need to take to break through your barriers. Then you can begin clearing the path to your success.

Receiving the EY Entrepreneur Of the Year Award in Florida in 2018
(Author's Collection)

105

CHAPTER 7

Clearing the Path

If you can see your path laid out in front of you step by step, you know it's not your path. Your own path you make with every step you take. That's why it's your path.
—JOSEPH CAMPBELL, AUTHOR OF *THE HERO'S JOURNEY*

Three questions haunted me for half my life:

1. "Why did we lose the Vietnam war?"

2. "Why did my father choose to stay behind?"

3. "What would have happened to me if we had won the war?"

As far as the first question was concerned, I learned everything I could about the Vietnam War. I was an incredibly well-read Marine, consuming every book about the Vietnam War I could get my hands on—even fiction. But the South Vietnamese view was missing from everything I read. What I truly wanted was my dad's perspective—but for the longest time, we were separated, no idea if he was living or not.

Hollywood tried to define our side of the war. So did historians and politicians, but I knew better.

For this reason, the second question couldn't be answered at all. I had my guesses, especially after I joined the military myself. But there had been plenty of other South Vietnamese soldiers who had left Vietnam with their families. So why did my dad decide to stay?

The third question was pure speculation. One of those "what if" questions that you know doesn't do you any good to dwell on, yet you can't help but play out different alternative histories in your mind.

We all do this. We all wonder "what if," circling our regrets and trauma like vultures. "What if I had been chosen for the promotion?" "What if I had studied more?" "What if I had stuck it out?"

People like to say, "Leave the past in the past. Move on. Don't reopen old wounds." Usually these words are offered as well-intentioned advice. The idea is that you have to move forward to make progress, that you can't clear the path by looking backward.

The problem is that the advice fails to acknowledge how the past can be a cage. And no amount of looking forward will get you out of the cage. What you need is the key. Only then can you move forward.

Where my Vietnam syndrome was concerned, I thought I had left everything in the past once I served my new country. In my mind, I had paid my debts to the US. And yet these questions kept haunting me. They became my personal hang-up, keeping me from fully clearing the professional path ahead of me.

When I was reunited with my father in 1992, you would think that would have been my chance to put those questions to rest—especially the question of why he chose to stay.

But when he began adjusting to life in the US, I thought to myself, *It's not the time. He needs to settle in.* I put off the conversation.

CHAPTER 7: CLEARING THE PATH

When I started pharmaceutical sales, I busied myself with learning everything I could to be a better salesman, putting in the hours. The conversation continued to be delayed. In my mind, I always made the argument it wasn't the right time for such a serious conversation.

In 2000, I was at the start of my entrepreneurial career, working to get MyDrugRep.com off the ground. Dad went back to Vietnam to visit his family there—and suddenly fell ill. He was rushed back to the US and was diagnosed with cancer, undergoing treatment immediately.

If ever I was going to talk with him about why he chose to stay behind in Vietnam, this should have been it. But I continued to delay, busying myself with work and justifying that he was already going through enough with treatment—I shouldn't add on the stress.

A few months into radiation therapy, he experienced a stroke and was rushed to the ER. The doctors gave him a slim chance to live.

I rushed from work to the ER, feeling completely helpless. This man who had been my role model, my hero, lay motionless in the bed. We had lost him once already. With my pharmaceutical training, I knew that if he was given certain drugs, there was a possibility the effects could be reversed.

He was given Coumadin or warfarin, the industry standard blood thinner, but in the end, he never woke up.

For eight years, I could have talked with him about my personal hang-ups, but I never took the chance. Now he was gone, and I'd never be able to ask him. At his funeral, he was buried with full military honors, and the South Vietnamese flag was presented to me by his fellow veterans.

You might think this moment of grief would be the final impetus needed to move me forward. But it wasn't. All I could think of were the years I had wasted—burying myself with remorse and regret.

Strange as it sounds, it would take a conservative, draft-dodging TV personality's rant to spur me on.

Closure

Though it sounds counterintuitive, sometimes you *need* the emotional trigger to spur you on to find closure. Which is exactly what happened to me during the 2004 presidential election. One day I was watching Fox News to see Bill O'Reilly talking about how Democratic candidate John Kerry had served in Vietnam but then came back to the US to protest the war.

That wasn't the part that riled me up, though. What got me were the disparaging remarks he made about the South Vietnamese military. During the televised interview with President George W. Bush, O'Reilly made statements that the South Vietnamese didn't deserve freedom. Why? Because they hadn't *fought* for it.[10]

My heart sank. Fury rose. My grief over the loss of my father resurrected. How dare this man say we hadn't fought for our freedom! Over a quarter million South Vietnamese died fighting for freedom. In contrast, it's estimated that up to seventy thousand Americans died in the Revolutionary War, combining deaths from battle, disease, and imprisonment. We fought like hell.

The interview made me see how the lack of closure—those unanswered questions—were holding me back. The key to unlocking my cage was to put in the effort to find the answers. My dad was gone, yes, but there was still opportunity for me to gain a South Vietnamese military perspective of the war.

---

10 Andrew Lam, "Opinion: Vietnamese Fondness for McCain Belies His Record," MercuryNews.com, October 28, 2008, https://www.mercurynews.com/2008/10/29/opinion-vietnamese-fondness-for-mccain-belies-his-record/.

CHAPTER 7: CLEARING THE PATH

This led me to writing my first book. I tracked down the people who had served with my dad: other South Vietnamese veterans and their American advisors, and anyone else willing to share their experience. In this way, I was able to make peace with the first question—why we had lost the war.

During the course of my research, I was connected with a journalist who had interviewed my father for a book that was never finished. He sent me the tapes of the interviews with Dad, and in those recordings, I heard my father's voice answer my second question:

"My plan was always to leave and rejoin the family," he said. "But as an officer, I have my honor and my duty. I could not leave too early. I have responsibilities."

As a Marine, those words hit me hard. Of course my dad had stayed back. He had a country to defend. Even though all appeared to be lost. He was the type who would stay to the bitter end. But as the interview continued, he added another thought to this:

"If I had left with the family when they did, maybe [Q] would not have turned out the way he did."

When he said those words, there was pride in his voice. Pride that I had gone into the service and followed in his footsteps as a pilot, defending the underdogs. With those words, I finally had the emotional closure the ten-year-old refugee inside of me needed.

As for the last question, it was always going to be conjecture. From piecing together the research and interviews, I came to the conclusion that had the war ended differently, then Vietnam would have likely ended up like another Korea—perpetually divided and at war, North against South. More than likely, I would have been drafted into the South Vietnamese military, compelled to serve rather than it being my own choice as it was in the US.

Beyond that, my life would have looked completely different. My professional opportunities would have been more limited. I would never have met so many people who have enriched my life. When I came to terms with this fact, I was watching my young daughter sleep, realizing she would never have come into the world had circumstances been different.

With these three hang-ups resolved, I found closure—no longer haunted by the past. The cage was opened, the path was cleared, the underdog unleashed.

At some point, you will have to confront your past. You cannot avoid it forever. You have to make peace with your past before you can move on. Better to do so on your own terms.

When you lack closure, your identity is locked up. It's unclear because you have mixed feelings about who you are and how you want to live. Finding closure is an essential part of the process if you're going to define success. Closure doesn't happen on its own—you have to put in the efforts to make it happen.

Have that tough conversation. Don't put it off like I did with my father. Neither of us was ready to talk about it during his life. He wrote about it on his own—and so did I. But we never processed the emotions together. There will never be a right time to do so. The right time is now.

Maybe it's a past trauma you have buried deep. Maybe it's the sibling you don't talk to, or some other estranged family member. Don't let your feelings devolve into regrets later in life.

You might need to start with writing. No one has to see it—but start writing your questions and researching the answers. You'll build the courage to then speak with others. Writing my first book did a lot to clear my path.

Learn to appreciate what you have more than what you've lost. Having my daughter helped me reframe all the circumstances of my life. She is the destiny that resulted from the coincidences. My ex-wife and I had tried for years to get pregnant, and I became a father late in life, but the light and joy she has brought is unmatched. Even the pain of the divorce was worth it to know she is in the world.

Because closure can bring you something you might not expect. Not only healing from your past, but an open door for your future.

Turn Closure into an Open Door

Maybe you've heard the saying "When God closes one door, he opens another." Well, it's true for closure too. When you are able to bring closure to your past, you simultaneously open up opportunities for yourself.

At my dad's funeral, there was nothing but regret for me. Regret I hadn't talked with him about Vietnam, yes, but also regrets over how his life had ended. He was always a fighter. For him to fight and survive the prison camps for so long only to succumb to the world's top killer—without an alternative treatment—felt like an immense injustice.

Now I had a new hang-up requiring closure. I kept wondering, *What if another drug had been available? Could he still be with us?*

While some people will say it's not worth lingering on such thoughts, the need for closure around those questions eventually led me to where I am today with my new company, Cadrenal Therapeutics. As I'm writing this, we're advancing a drug called tecarfarin, a new anticoagulant that can serve as an alternative to warfarin, or Coumadin, the longtime standard for blood thinners and one that was once used as a rat poison.

Without getting too technical, the inspiration behind the drug is strongly related to my father's death. There is a subset of people with rare cardiovascular conditions, and warfarin doesn't serve these people. In fact, with such patients, it can actually increase the risk of stroke. I'll never know for sure, of course, and I know the ER doctors were doing their best for my father when he was rushed to the hospital.

The pain I experienced with my father's loss has turned into an opportunity—not just a business opportunity but an opportunity to spare others the same pain and loss. That's what motivates us every day as we go through the arduous process of clinical trials and FDA approval.

No doubt tecarfarin is an underdog drug, passed over by Big Pharma and their arsenal of Eliquis and Xarelto. Cadrenal Therapeutics is an underdog startup—but that's also our greatest asset.

When you look back at your professional journey thus far, you likely have regrets. Maybe it was the job you were laid off from. Maybe the promotion you didn't receive. Or the job you wish you hadn't taken. In all of these, finding closure can help you create your next opportunity. You can rise again like a phoenix.

Walt Disney was fired from his first newspaper job for "lacking imagination." Sara Blakely was rejected by every manufacturer and retailer she spoke to before she founded Spanx on her own. Steven Spielberg was turned down by the USC School of Cinematic Arts—several times. Vera Wang failed to achieve her dream of being an Olympic figure skater. On and on we can go.

All these success stories have one thing in common: they were underdogs. They applied their underdog drive to turn closure into an opportunity.

You might say, "But I'm not any of those people." No, you're not. But neither were they when they started. They became successes not because of their names or backgrounds but because they focused on effort and results time after time.

Ask yourself, "What can I create from the ashes?"

Look at the times in your life when you feel a lack of closure. Study them. How can they be turned into opportunities?

For instance, have you ever left a job over a toxic boss? Then you have experience related to developing a healthy corporate culture. How might you monetize that skill?

What is a hobby or sport you used to play? Use it to create common ground with your next prospect or interview.

No one can replicate your exact experience. All your experience is on the table—good, bad, and ugly—to create common ground and opportunities.

Time after time, my experience in the Marines has helped me connect with investors, potential board members, and prospects. My experience as a refugee has led to speaking opportunities and was a major factor in the interest for my first book.

You can't control the cards you've been dealt. But the best way to find closure isn't to fold your hand. It's to play the cards. Win, lose, draw, you're still in the game. Only by playing your cards can you turn coincidence into destiny. Be at the table, all the time. Be in the game. Be in the fight.

Mental Stamina

Everything described here requires immense mental stamina. And if you're going to clear the path, you have to be mentally tough to make decisions whenever you're physically exhausted. And that's where many people fail. They let their body make the decision for them rather than their mind.

Your mental stamina directly impacts whether you put in the effort. You'll always have mental stressors in your life outside of your job, whether it's parenting, a strained marriage, financial responsibilities, illness. Fill in the blank with your situation. All of these require massive amounts of time and energy.

Mental stamina is about knowing when you're feeling out of whack. It is forward thinking to fight complacency. It recognizes that you are replaceable—even when it's the company you built.

This was an approach I had to learn in the military. We were taught that everyone is replaceable. It might be your seat in the cockpit today, but it's not guaranteed tomorrow. Whether it's because the enemy gets you or you fail to live up to standards, no one is ever truly indispensable.

The only way to fight this is through your effort—being known as the one who brings value. And even if you're already doing so, then do the extra you need to do so you'll be safe apart from the job. If you had to leave your job today—whether by the company's choice or your own—would you be okay?

If the answer is no, then define the efforts needed to make yourself okay. This goes back to self-awareness around your situation. Are you able to be mobile if needed? Can you afford to strike out on your own if you don't have a single paying client for six-plus months?

For example, I once had an incredible job offer from GE Medical Systems—more money, more influence. On the surface, it appeared to be in the right direction for the success I had defined. But I would have had to move to Minneapolis. That was a no-go for me, so I turned the card over quickly. And believe me, doing so required a ton of mental toughness.

Be aware of your environment, your industry, and where the jobs are headed if you were to be displaced. For instance, when Elon

CHAPTER 7: **CLEARING THE PATH**

Musk decided to move Tesla's HQ to Austin, it forced a reckoning for thousands of employees: Uproot their lives to Texas? Or forfeit their job to stay in California?

Shareholders might only look at how a company's decisions impact the bottom line, but the real bottom line is that these big corporate moves affect real people just like you every day. When you don't own the company, you will have to be prepared and mentally tough to make your go/no-go decision. If that sounds daunting, it's meant to be. You have to be daunted so you can develop the resilience to survive and thrive.

Even if you do own the company, you'll still need the mental stamina to make those go/no-go decisions. You'll have to close some doors to open others. And there will always be repercussions—or results—from those efforts.

Just like with a long-distance race, you don't build up mental stamina overnight. It's a process. The more situations where you have to be mentally tough, the more resilience you develop, the more stamina. You'll be more prepared for the journey ahead.

If success means being able to finish a marathon, it's not a matter of luck. There's a formula for finishing. You have to be prepared for the unknown—the weather, how you'll feel that day, and any circumstances that might occur during the race, like a pulled muscle or a hole in your shoe that suddenly appears.

Many people go out too fast in their first marathon and end up walking the last 6.2 miles—or dropping out. They didn't pace themselves. They didn't follow the nutrition and training plan.

When looking to improve my marathon time, I studied the winner in my age group who had run twenty minutes faster than me. I discovered we were about the same in terms of height, weight, and age. But where we were different is that I had put in thirty-five to forty miles a week, and he was training sixty-five miles a week. Now I knew how to adjust my efforts.

It's the same with golf. You can't do the same stuff every time you go out on the course and expect different results. That's the insanity cycle. You have to build up the mental stamina. You have to learn how to adjust your mental approach to different types of weather and ground conditions. Practice doesn't make perfect, but it does make progress.

Reflaction—Reframe Negative Experiences

In 2020, I faced two of my greatest challenges—and it wasn't COVID. In my personal life, I went through a divorce, and in my professional life, my company was dissolved. The two weren't related to each other at all, but those were the cards I was dealt that year, a year of isolation. I'll discuss the dissolution more in the next chapter, so to help you with this particular reflection, I'll give you an example from my divorce.

My ex-wife and I actually met as a result of my profession—which is one example of why you can never totally separate personal and professional. We met at a healthcare convention in Las Vegas, both of us entrepreneurs. Like so many couples experience, we grew apart over time as we became different people. We did counseling, tried to work through our issues, but in the end, we both agreed the only way to clear our path was to find closure on the marriage.

By going about it this way, we were able to turn the pain into a path forward. We developed a plan to co-parent our daughter so that she wouldn't have to move, and we have even gone on vacations together.

Both of us could have walked away. Instead, we found the closure to create an opportunity. We reframed the negative experience and found our destinations. Our daughter is now in her first year in college.

Much of clearing your path comes down to being able to reframe negative experiences. That's true for finding closure, and it's true for developing your mental stamina. One of the greatest lessons you can learn in youth and amateur sports is to have good sportsmanship—even when you've just been crushed or received a bad call from an official.

You can't control whether others act right on the court, but you are responsible for your own good conduct. Be willing to clean up the mess, whether it was your fault or not. Your job description may not say you're in charge, but you can always be in charge of your own efforts.

Never simply walk away from a situation. That's not closure. Learn from what happened and apply the lesson to the future. Find the good you can create from the ashes. And don't ever quit. I have never quit a marathon (sixteen starts, sixteen finishes), nor walked off the golf course due to a bad day.

How you reframe negative experiences will look different for you, of course, but there are a couple of exercises you can do to start the process:

First, do some writing. Write down some of your negative experiences and then write down something positive that came from them. If you can't identify a positive for every negative yet, that's okay. Focus on the ones you can identify and pay attention to how your mental stamina was developed as a result.

Look for patterns and then filter them through ER: effort and results. What can be replicated to make you more productive? Are there experiences that can even be monetized or transformed into opportunities? If so, how do those opportunities align with your definition of success?

Second, go out of your way to have coffee or lunch with someone different from you once this next week. Maybe they come from a different ethnic heritage, different faith, or a different political stance.

Look for the common ground throughout your conversation. By doing so, you'll not only build your rapport with that one individual but you'll gain valuable experience for connecting with other new people. You're clearing the path for the future.

The common ground in all human experience is pain. We all have pain in our past that we need closure from, but also pain that can create opportunities. By confronting the negative experiences, underdogs are able to move from losers to winners, from surviving to thriving.

AVENUE OF APPROACH 3

COURSE CORRECT

CHAPTER 8

From Loser to Winner

Failure is not the end, it's simply a stepping stone towards success.
—MIKE KRZYZEWSKI, A.K.A. COACH K

You might think my first taste of loss in life was the fall of Saigon. After all, you can't lose anything much bigger than your country. I can still see the tears of the other refugees as we listened to the announcement over the radio in that old Marine barracks on Guam.

The fall of Saigon was certainly bleak and uncertain. But the realization of all we lost didn't sink in until adulthood. Maybe because of my age, or maybe because we were in survival mode. Either way, I didn't feel like a loser when South Vietnam disappeared from the map.

My first sense of being a loser happened at my first Little League baseball game. Right away, I felt just how much of an outsider I was. One of the coaches asked me for my name, but after he failed to understand it several times, he gave up and said, "Whatever, I'll just call you Sam."

Then he stuck me out in right field, because—as I learned later—that's where you put a kid with no talent. A fly ball sped toward me,

I missed the catch in the lights, and the ball struck me so hard in the chest it knocked me to the ground.

Everyone laughed. The kids. The parents in the stands. The coach. Laughter.

I'd like to think it was the shock of the moment. Maybe it looked hilarious. Maybe I would have laughed if the situation had been reversed and I saw it from the stands. But back in Vietnam, I had been both a top student and athlete, playing soccer and badminton. I'd never felt this way before—helpless, useless, unworthy. Loser.

Being laughed at made me extremely uncomfortable. I took it as a challenge. In my mind, I said, *Let me show you,* and I dedicated my efforts to learning everything I could about baseball.

The kids were the first to come around me as a support system. They saw me working my tail off and welcomed me in, taught me the game. We practiced hitting tennis balls in the alley between our apartment buildings every night. The coach started driving me to and from practice since my mom couldn't do it, and likewise, he saw the effort I was putting forth.

The parents took longer to come around. I can sometimes still hear the jeers of "Hey Sam, are you going to get a hit at all this year?" and "Come on, Coach, keep him on the bench!" Not a single person in the crowd was there to cheer me on.

By the next spring, the story had changed. At our first practice game, I was the lead-off batter—and hit a homer over left field. Running around the bases, I could see the other parents' faces filled with disbelief. Was this really the same kid?

I started at second base that year and like something out of a movie, I hit the game-winning run in the league championship game. Because we were the champions, our coach then got to select the all-star team for our region. He ended up picking about five kids from our team for the all-star lineup—including me. The experience gave me so much confidence to see how putting in the effort translated into the results I wanted—a Little League All-Star from Saigon.

But I've also experienced going from winner to loser. After MyDrugRep, my next startup was Espero BioPharma. The business started off well, thanks to a partnership with a European supplier for two FDA-approved products that were generating cash flow.

The other arm of the business was drug development, where we were actively developing two other drugs. We were trying to do both the commercial and development side and, frankly, it was too much since we weren't the size of a company like Pfizer.

Ultimately, it was my decision to end the European partnership and focus all our efforts on drug development. Going into this decision, I knew it meant we would be shedding the side of the business that was generating cash flow and become dependent on investor funding.

The mistake I made was assuming that investors would see the move as lean and focused. Instead, they were confused as to why we dropped the part of the business actually making money—especially given the inherently risky nature of drug development. In short, my decision had made the company a riskier investment—and they weren't buying.

As our resources shrank, we turned our efforts to survival, including slashing my own salary to try to stay afloat. But in the end, the company had to be dissolved and the assets assigned to creditors. To this day, it's a loss that I've had to own—mentally and financially.

The good news is that's not where the story ended. From the ashes of Espero, Cadrenal was born. One of the two drugs we had been developing at Espero was tecarfarin. And because I had been honest with investors and creditors about the situation at Espero, I was able to maintain their trust when launching Cadrenal.

Using the lessons learned from Espero, we've been able to course correct, buy back the asset, and on January 24, 2023, Cadrenal Therapeutics made its debut on the Nasdaq. Not only was it the first biotech IPO of the year but one of the very few since September 2022. Ringing the bell to close a trading day is the kind of moment every American entrepreneur dreams about.

My life has gone from war to Wall Street, from loser to winner on multiple levels. The recurring theme has been a focus on effort and results. Underdogs have the uncanny ability to transform losses into wins. They never see loss as the end of the story but as a page to turn in a long game.

Finish What You Start

We need to fundamentally reframe what it means to be a winner versus a loser, especially when defining your own success. Ultimately, what makes you a winner is about how you handle failure. Do you walk away from it? Or do you confront it? How you react will determine your next act.

Let's go back to *Rocky* for a second. Early on in the movie, trainer Mickey calls Rocky a bum. He calls out Rocky for not giving his all to the sport, for ditching his talent by going to work for the local loan shark, Gazzo.

That label of "bum" hits Rocky harder than a punch from Apollo Creed. Just before his fight with Apollo, Rocky tells his girlfriend Adrian, "I can't beat him … I ain't even in the guy's league."

At first, this sounds like a defeatist attitude. This doesn't sound like a guy who has made a turnaround and is giving his best effort.

CHAPTER 8: FROM LOSER TO WINNER

But in typical underdog fashion, he reframes the situation by creating his own definition for success:

"It really don't matter if I lose this fight. It really don't matter if this guy opens my head, either. 'Cause all I wanna do is go the distance. Nobody's ever gone the distance with Creed, and if I can go that distance, you see, and that bell rings and I'm still standin', I'm gonna know for the first time in my life, see, that I weren't just another bum from the neighborhood."[11]

Even though he loses the fight, Rocky comes out of it a winner, not a loser. Why? Because he went the distance. He gave it his all and did what no one else had ever done before.

You can still be a winner, even in the midst of a failure. But it starts with a decision to course correct by finishing what you start.

My golfing buddies like to call me a "grinder," because I always give every match my all. Even when the results aren't what I hoped for, I still push to the last hole. Most people only define winning by the score on the card. And when that score isn't a number they like, they walk off the course prematurely, drop out, and go home. DNF for "did not finish" goes next to their names. For me, DNF is never an option unless I am physically hurt or have an emergency. Now, if I can win both ways—scoring and finishing—all the better!

You have to look at whether you're applying effort in the right environment. I know guys who pay good money for golf lessons and can do well in front of their instructor or on the driving range—but then they perform terribly in the tournament. Why? Because it's not just about the repetition—you need repetition in competition. Your efforts must be exerted in an environment where they can produce results.

---

11   *Rocky,* directed by Sylvester Stallone (1976, Philadelphia: Chartoff-Winkler Productions, Inc.).

Despite your best efforts, the results still may not be what you hoped for. When that happens, you can still course correct. For instance, you might miss your target time in the marathon, so you shift your efforts to finishing the race, practicing that last 10K with intention to keep up your race pace.

When most people think of course correcting, they think about switching from the wrong path to the right one. That's one type. But you might be on the right path and still need a mental course correction to reframe how you define success. So instead of thinking in terms of "winners and losers," we must think in terms of "finishers and dropouts."

Choose to see failure as an asset. Why? Because failure is an opportunity to course correct. It teaches you how to pivot. It creates a brand of motivation that perpetual winning can never do. And that's why underdogs are so powerful—because they have learned how to course correct by redefining success. But also by redefining failure.

Redefining Failure

While baseball is considered America's favorite pastime, the sport was heavily influenced by British games like cricket and rounders. Basketball, however, is a uniquely American sport. Dr. James Naismith is credited as the inventor during his tenure at the YMCA International Training School (now Springfield College) in Springfield, Massachusetts, developing the game in the 1890s.[12]

The sport spread fast across the nation—and then the world. By 1936, it had enough international appeal to be included in the

---

12 Springfield College, "Where Basketball Was Invented: The History of Basketball," Springfield.edu, accessed October 24, 2024, https://springfield.edu/about/birthplace-of-basketball/.

CHAPTER 8: FROM LOSER TO WINNER

Summer Olympics. The US men's basketball team has won gold in every single Summer Olympics with three notable exceptions:

In 1980, when the US boycotted the Moscow games; in 1988, when the US took bronze after being defeated in the semifinal round by the Soviet Union; and in 2004, when the US took bronze again after being defeated in the semifinal round by Argentina.

With the benefit of hindsight, we can almost dismiss the 1988 loss. The Soviet Union was using professional-level athletes at a time when professionals were still barred from competing on the Olympic level. And from what we know now, the Soviet athletes likely had an extra "boost."

When professionals were finally permitted to compete at the Olympics, it led to the US's 1992 Dream Team featuring the likes of Charles Barkley, Patrick Ewing, Larry Bird, Magic Johnson, and, of course, Michael Jordan.

The truly shocking case is 2004. In the first round of tournament play, the US was soundly defeated by Puerto Rico by a whopping nineteen points—the largest margin of loss for the US ever at the Olympics. And while the team managed to scrape by with a bronze, the tournament was considered an embarrassment for them.

Things didn't look much better at the 2006 FIBA World Championship when the team walked away with another bronze. As the 2008 Olympics approached, Team USA men's basketball was entering the tournament for the first time in underdog territory.

Team USA made a major course correction. They brought in a new team coach—Mike Krzyzewski, a.k.a. Coach K, who had led the Duke Blue Devils to five national titles—and the late Kobe Bryant was named as team captain.

Several of the 2004 team members returned for 2008, including LeBron James and Dwyane Wade, who had been coming off their

129

rookie year back in 2004. Now a little older and wiser, the weight of failure gave them and the rest of the team renewed motivation. They didn't want to repeat the same mistakes. They wanted redemption.

The culture of the team itself shifted. They weren't told to forget and move on from 2004 but to shift the narrative. And the gold medal they ended up winning was all the more valuable for it. A photo from the medal ceremony showed Coach K standing in the middle of the team, wearing all twelve gold medals—their way of honoring him for helping the team redefine failure.

Besides the quote at the top of this chapter, Coach K has two others that stand out to me in the context of course correcting failure:

- "You have to play like you are in first place, even when you are not."

- "Success is a result of relentless preparation and tenacious effort."

Notice with that second quote he says nothing about success being defined by winning the game. If you put in relentless preparation and tenacious effort, then the result is success. If you play like you are in first place even when you're not, then you course correct failure.

Coach K is the only basketball coach who has coached three teams to Olympic gold, because he redefined success by what was happening on the court, not the scoreboard.

In 1986, I met Coach John Wooden at his book signing of *They Call Me Coach* during my third year at UCLA. My favorite quote from him remains "Success is peace of mind which is a direct result of self-satisfaction in knowing you did your best to become the best you are capable of becoming."

The psychology behind failure is fascinating. Many athletes have spoken similarly about being more motivated by the fear of failure than the desire of winning. No one wins all the time, so they do whatever they can to avoid the experience of defeat. They put in the preparation, the effort, knowing the results will follow.

In the last section, we talked about taking your negative experiences and finding the positive in them, whether that was an unexpected outcome or a lesson. Likewise, failure should be examined not only as an experience but also through the filter of your effort and results.

Seen through this lens, failure allows you to course correct rather than become a part of your identity. Never let failure define you. Redefine failure as something to be grateful for.

Gratitude

It sounds ridiculous to be grateful for failure. But if failure teaches you to be more dedicated, as it did with the 2008 Olympic basketball team, then it becomes a source for gratitude. If failure makes you more resilient, then it becomes a source of gratitude. If failure teaches you the greatest lesson of your career, then it becomes a source of gratitude.

Dropouts see themselves as victims of failure. What they actually fail in is not the task itself but taking ownership of how their efforts played a role. They fail to recalculate and course correct.

Finishers—and underdogs—see failure through the lens of gratitude. They take ownership of their effort and results to recalculate and course correct.

Gratitude is always aligned with ownership. It's impossible to be grateful for something that isn't yours. You may be grateful for your family, your friends, your home, your accomplishments, your job—*because* they are yours. You might be respectful of or impressed by what someone else owns, but you're not grateful for what they have.

One of the rules I've followed with every startup I've had is to make sure I have skin in the game. When you have personal ownership in the failure or success of a business, it becomes much more difficult to drop out. You're far more grateful for what you create.

This is another concept I see play out on the golf course. The players who take ownership of their effort and results also have the highest levels of sportsmanship. They don't lose their cool when they have a bad hole. They're grateful for the experience, learn from it, and don't continually make the same mistakes. They don't get embarrassed by their poor scores that everyone can see.

Gratitude paired with failure develops a growth mindset. Instead of wallowing in the pain, you can move forward by adapting and adopting.

Let's face it—this is easier said than done. For driven people, failure is psychologically damaging. When you have a high sense of ownership for something, the loss stings more. Especially if you recognize that your own efforts contributed to the problem.

When that happens, it will be more difficult to be grateful in the moment. It may feel impossible. You'll be tempted to throw in the towel and drop out. And that's when you'll need some extra support.

Reflaction—Support Systems

No one goes from loser to winner on their own. No one can be resilient alone. Especially on the heels of a loss or disappointment, you need support systems to help pull you through.

All these years later, I'm grateful for how the kids on my baseball team became a support system for me, especially since my mom couldn't attend the games. In the Marine Corps, I had a half dozen peers who operated as my "step siblings." Since we weren't in the same units and therefore not competing for the same ranks or ratings, we

CHAPTER 8: **FROM LOSER TO WINNER**

could bounce ideas off each other and support one another fully from across the country or the world. But I also made sure to have someone in the mix who was a rank or two above me—someone like Doug Hamlin who could give me a more experienced perspective.

Often, people think of support systems in terms of whom they can vent to and have a sympathetic ear with. But in reality, you need the people who will hold you accountable, challenge you, and push you. I've always worked hard to fill the boards of my companies with CEOs—people with immense credibility who can offer up wisdom and counsel and not just with their past credentials.

While you may have a mix of support systems made up of friends, family, or colleagues, the key here is to have a support network built on expertise. When I wanted to improve my running, I found a running coach—someone with ten years more experience than me and who competed on a national level. He not only had experience in terms of knowledge but also *action*—he actively practiced what he preached.

For Rocky, it was Mickey. For the "Redeem Team," it was Coach K. Ideally, you need someone who is in the game. Engineer your support systems around skills and experience the same way a coach builds their roster.

Start with the following roles:

- **The Peer**—someone who is at the same stage as you but not in competition with you.

- **The Big Brother/Sister**—someone who is a step or two ahead of you so you can learn from their mistakes.

- **The Industry Peer**—someone who is in your industry but not in direct competition with you.

133

- **The Outsider**—someone who has experience completely different from you and, therefore, can provide you an outsider's perspective and help you find the blind spots.

You don't need a table full of generalists but specialists. That way, when you need sales advice, you have a sales expert to call on. If you need strategy advice, you talk with a CEO. And keep in mind you will need a pinch hitter to sub in for special situations. As your circumstances change, or as you course correct, you may need to rotate people in and out.

Depending on where you are on your journey, you'll also need one more role to fill: the Advancer. These are the contributors who will not only support you but actively advance your mission. They will be your most supportive investors, your loyal board chair, and your greatest cheerleader. They make calls and things happen.

With a great support system, you can accelerate your growth. You can change losses into wins. And you can brighten even the darkest days.

CHAPTER 9

Overcoming the Darkest Days

Out of life's school of war—what doesn't kill me, makes me stronger.
—FRIEDRICH NIETZSCHE, *TWILIGHT OF THE IDOLS*

In March 1991, Kuwait was officially liberated, and President George H.W. Bush declared, "The ghosts of Vietnam have been laid to rest beneath the sands of the Arabian desert." Whether that was true or not is debatable, but it certainly aligned with my own feelings of laying my personal Vietnam syndrome to rest.

And yet the darkest days of my military career happened over a year later in August of 1992. I was deployed for the second time to the Persian Gulf, embarked on the USS *Tarawa* as a helicopter aircraft commander. Many of the flights were completed at night, utilizing night vision goggles to make the deck landing—high level of difficulty.

In the first two weeks of deployment back to Kuwait, there were consecutive crashes with the pilots killed during training missions. We had zero casualties in the Gulf War, and now we had three dead in the span of a week's time.

First, we had to contend with the deaths. Even though I wasn't involved in the crashes myself, these were my squadron mates, my Marine brothers. Any one of us could have been in those seats, so it was a massive blow to the unit's morale.

Next, we had to face the unknown of what would come next. The Admiral grounded our entire unit and ordered the amphibious carrier pulled back to Bahrain. We were there for three weeks while investigations were conducted. When you're grounded, it's no vacation either. We weren't flying, and time stood still in the heat of the Persian Gulf and the deadly Arabian desert.

Clearly, something dangerous was happening. My feeling was that the checks and balances weren't happening like they should—but who would be next to fly and find out? Can you still go out and fly when your comrades have just died?

In the end, the three top officers were all relieved of duty and replaced with new officers. Losing our leadership in such an unprecedented way was another massive blow to morale. And then we still had to hope the underlying problem had been solved as we were cleared to fly again and project America's power at the tip of the spear.

When you've been out of the cockpit for as long as we were, you have to be requalified for flight duty by a qualified and current pilot. On my requalification flight, I was so nervous my hands were shaking. Once I was requalified, it was then my duty to go back up in the air with other members of the unit to get them requalified.

This is a major differentiator between the military and the private sector. In pharmaceuticals, if a drug develops a safety problem, it can be recalled. If FDA trials go awry, you can always kill the drug and cut your losses. If a job is treating you poorly, you can resign and move on.

Not so much in the Marines. You have a mission to fulfill, orders to follow. You don't get to resign from your job while deployed or at war. You don't get to ask for a day off or request PTO. When your number's called, you better be ready. Your buddies are counting on you. Don't ever let them down.

Likewise, you don't get to quit the darkest days when they come. You don't get to quit difficulty or setbacks. We all have to face them.

"Don't dismount when riding a tiger" is an idiom from Vietnamese folklore that refers to finding yourself in a bad situation you can't get out of. Riding a tiger is dangerous—but getting off is even more so. When the darkest days come, you have no choice but to ride them out—because if you try to jump off, they'll consume you.

The darkest days don't have to define you, but they *are* pivotal. What matters most is the next step. How do you overcome the darkest days? What are the course corrections you have to make after defeat?

Recognition and Resilience

Earlier we discussed how emotional triggers don't announce themselves—they are subconscious, capable of rearing up in unexpected moments. Your darkest days will have emotional triggers attached to them, but the events themselves live in the past. They're not subconscious at all. They exist in your mind, marked like bright yellow caution tape cordoning off a crime scene.

No one necessarily wants to revisit their darkest days. However, they tend to get darker as a consequence of ignoring them. You cannot overcome an obstacle if you are not first able to recognize its presence.

You might think that's obvious—but it's not always. We don't always recognize our darkest days the moment they are happening. Remember, when my family boarded the plane that night to leave Vietnam, I thought it was temporary. Only a week later did the permanence of the situation begin to sink in.

Other times, you're hyperaware you're in the midst of the darkest days. This was the case for me with the aftermath of the helicopter crashes in my second deployment, the dissolution of Espero, and my father's death.

The darkest days become milestones—markers of the changing seasons in life, crossroad moments that compel you to make go/no-go decisions. They force you to decide whether you're going to jump ship or help bail the water out.

Most people are "on the fence people." They have no strategic plan for their lives, so they straddle. That's the beauty of the darkest days—they *push* you off the fence. Once you fall, then you have the choice to get up. You have the choice of resilience.

Failing to recognize the darkest days means forgoing resilience. You don't become resilient from the comfortable times but from the uncomfortable times.

The darkest days often happen as the result of coincidences you can't control. And sometimes they result from a poor decision. Either way, resilience is the destiny you create through your efforts.

Even though you can't plan when the darkest days occur, you can make a resilience plan. You have a choice in your response. You have the choice to become stronger.

Recognize that the darkest days put you in a physical and mental state of stress, confusion, and conflict. The worst response is to say "I'm fine." Your body and mind know better, no matter what you say.

We've talked already about the importance of preparation, and it's no different with the darkest days. Even though you don't know when they will come, you know they *will* come. So make sure you're making preparations in the following areas:

FINANCIAL HEALTH

How healthy are you financially? For most people, their resiliency plan is dependent on how much is in their savings. The number there dictates your runway for self-sufficiency, whether you lose your job, start up a company, experience an emergency, or have to alter your life circumstances.

PHYSICAL HEALTH

How is your physical health? When the darkest days come, you might not be in a position to focus much on your physical well-being, so are you taking care of yourself now? Are you eating well, exercising, and getting enough sleep? Your health will help you weather the storm and bounce back faster.

SOCIAL HEALTH

Have you established a support network for yourself? Who can you depend on to be there for you when the darkest days come? Don't let your whole social circle be based on work. If the company moves you to a new location—or lets you go—suddenly you could find yourself without anyone to lean on.

You've got to cover these three bases in your resilience plan, along with any others specific to your circumstances. For instance, your mental and emotional health. If you've learned what your emotional triggers are, then you can be better prepared for them to reveal themselves. Some people rely on their faith, so perhaps you also consider your spiritual health.

During the darkest days, there's no window of time for you to scramble and pull these together. Preparing these areas of your life is a recognition that the hard times will come. And you'll be better primed for resiliency.

When I was simultaneously going through my divorce and the dissolution of Espero during the 2020 pandemic, I'm so grateful I had these in place. Even with everything going on, I was still running three or four times a week, which allowed me to release much of the stress I was carrying. My finances were in order even though I had to take huge pay cuts as the company was winding down, which also resulted in the loss of over $1 million of my "skin in the game" money. And my friends and mentors were available to provide encouragement and counsel as needed.

Was it a difficult year? Of course. But it could have been far more difficult without a resiliency plan in place. Recognizing the darkest days means taking the effort to be prepared. Resilience will be the result.

The Three Paths

What do you do when the darkest days involve defeat? What are your options to move forward?

You'll find three paths to take on the other side of defeat. How you approach the juncture will determine which path you will take. When it comes to professional defeats, you first have to learn how to separate your personal worth from the setbacks. "Loser" doesn't have to be your identity because you get to choose your identity.

For instance, unlike other darkest days in my life, the dissolution of Espero was rooted in a decision I had made. It was ultimately my call to shift directions with the company. In the aftermath, I could have made excuses or blamed others. But failing to recognize the facts would have prevented resilience.

CHAPTER 9: OVERCOMING THE DARKEST DAYS

We had to face the fact that we didn't get the results we wanted, so we adjusted our next efforts. By notifying creditors, we avoided bankruptcy and didn't have to terminate the FDA programs for the drugs we were developing.

Life had given me enough experience to remind me that Espero was not the core of my identity. Thousands of biotech and pharma companies have failed. Espero was operating in a high-risk, high-return, high-failure-rate industry.

And yet no one lost their life when Espero closed down. I still had a place to sleep. I still had my health, my daughter, my friends and community. And because I had been transparent with the creditors, investors, banks, and regulators, I still had my reputation. You can't put a price on any of those.

To think of my life like a tree, the company was not the trunk or roots—it was a single branch. Yes, it hurt when the brand was cut off. I'd had high hopes that it would bear fruit. But the tree could still live without the branch. With time and tending, new branches could be grown. And since Espero went through an organized wind down rather than an outright collapse, the result was that creditors believed in me when I said I wanted to give tecarfarin another chance.

So if you find yourself in a similar circumstance, start by reframing the defeat. With the right perspective of the defeat, you'll be better prepared when the three paths present themselves to you.

On the other side of defeat, let gratitude become your superpower. In the midst of loss, underdogs move by focusing on what they do have. Fixating on what you've lost keeps you in a victim mentality. By separating your self-worth from the setback, you can move forward and take the right path.

That said, what are the three paths you can take on the other side of defeat?

PATH 1: DROPPING OUT

Remember, in reframing how we see winners and losers, it's more helpful to think of the two more in terms of finishers and dropouts. Part of why I prefer *dropout* to the term *quit* is that there are certainly healthy times to quit.

An exercise many C-suites and entrepreneurs practice is to analyze what they should start, quit, and keep doing. If a venture or activity is not beneficial to the company, it should be terminated. Same on the individual level. If a habit or approach is not helping your financial, physical, or social health, then it should be quit. This is *positive quitting*.

Dropping out, on the other hand, is when you stop doing what you should be doing. It's a choice to abandon the success you've defined. Those who drop out don't settle for status quo—they dive into *status woe*.

These are the people who live in the "if only …" for the rest of their lives. Instead of going to the ER by looking at their effort and results, they abandon the course altogether. They live in a state of victimhood and blame everything and everyone for their lack of success. They give all the power over to their coincidences and take no power over their destiny.

PATH 2: RETURN TO STATUS QUO

The people who return to the status quo do so because they would rather live with the devil they know than face the unknown. In the context of Vietnam, these were the people we knew who initially fled the country but then chose to return and live under the Communist regime.

In the professional sphere, these are the people who might start out on the path of their defined success, but after a few setbacks, they return to what they know best. For instance, this might be the person who started up their own business but, in light of the challenges, chooses to return to the safer corporate world.

For some people, returning to the status quo could be the right move. They're still choosing between two difficult choices, but they have at least taken some time to recalculate the math and determine they would rather pour their efforts into what they know best. With the right approach, status quo may offer some the opportunity to recalibrate and rejuvenate.

The problem is that the status quo becomes comfortable, and once you're comfortable, you can become complacent. You may slip into letting others define success for you. So if you find yourself reverting to status quo, give yourself a deadline, because there is still an opportunity for you to jump over to the third path.

PATH 3: DIG DEEPER

The third path is for the underdogs. These are the people who learn from their defeat, go to the ER to analyze their effort and results, and then make the proper adjustments. On the surface, it may first appear like they are returning to the status quo. Perhaps they go back to their old job—but what you don't see is they are using that as a time to reset, gain new skills, and develop the resources they need to try again.

They are digging deeper to unleash their underdog energy. It may take time, but they are looking for the right tools to reignite the ashes and bring the phoenix to life.

This is exactly what happened for me on the other side of Espero. Nothing was wasted because in our shift toward drug development, I had learned about *orphan drug designation*. This is a special regulatory status granted to any drugs that can help prevent or treat a rare condition or disease affecting fewer than two hundred thousand people in the US.

When Espero was dissolved, one of the drugs we had been developing was tecarfarin, an anticoagulant designed to help a subset of patients with rare conditions be spared from heart attacks, strokes, and death caused by other treatments. My personal draw to the drug was deeply connected to my father's death and the lingering question "Could this have saved him?"

As an asset of the company, the drug had gone into receivership. However, because I still had the trust of the creditors from how Espero was handled, we were able to buy back the drug and obtain an additional orphan drug designation so that clinical trials could proceed under the new company, Cadrenal Therapeutics.

Every underdog, whether in history or in fiction, has taken this third path. They have dug deeper to take the road less traveled, to think outside the box, and to find their way back to success.

The worst thing you can do is sit around, waiting for your fate to be decided by others. There's no path forward, and you're worse off than the people who drop out or return to the status quo. On the other side of defeat, don't take a breather—take action. Take a hard look at your effort and results and ask, "What happened?" With the answers you find, you can pivot and persist.

Pivotal Persistence

You'll find two types of persistence in the world—intelligent and unintelligent. Unintelligent or annoying persistence is the type you see in the pestering salesperson who won't stop to see you don't need—or want—what they're selling. They push and push, sounding like

CHAPTER 9: **OVERCOMING THE DARKEST DAYS**

a script, and become a thorn in your side. They call and text you endlessly and send you unsolicited LinkedIn messages.

The best salespeople are intelligently persistent. These are the ones who are targeted and selective in who they approach with their products or services. They are great communicators—especially with their listening skills. Their resilience combined with respect allow them to overcome objections by putting the other person's needs first.

In the world of startup fundraising, people say no more than yes, so you automatically have to develop a skill for persistence. You have to learn what people care about and what is in their best interest, not just yours. If you want to avoid pestering, then the answer is to center your persistence on what is right for others.

Intelligent persistence isn't always about IQ but sometimes about EQ. Major John Braddon didn't have to turn back for my dad. It would have been smarter—and completely justified—for him to keep moving with the Marines he was responsible for. And yet he knew that turning back was the right thing to do. In 2005, at my first book launch, he told me, "When your dad was supporting US Marines, he became one of us. I never hesitated to return to rescue him."

Likewise, my dad didn't have to stay and fight to the bitter end of the war. It would have been smarter for him to leave with us. But as an officer, he stayed out of his sense of duty and moral responsibility.

It would have been more logical for my mother to move us to France. But she knew it was right to take us to the US instead. She put her own comfort second to what she believed was best for her children.

The US government only planned to evacuate about five thousand American personnel and their dependents from Saigon. In the end, they evacuated and resettled over two million South Vietnamese from a sense of moral responsibility. That's why I love our country! Even in the midst of a disappointing result, do the extra.

Intelligent persistence pivots on what the right efforts are, not always what the most logical or smartest efforts would be. But you can't know what that is if you haven't defined success through the lens of your purpose and values.

The darkest days may force you to pivot—but you must always pivot from what you know to be right. You can never effectively pivot without an anchor point, and you get to choose where that anchor point lies.

The pivot may not look intelligent to anyone else. In fact, it may look like the most dangerous course of action. It may look like you're riding a tiger.

But sometimes the tiger's back is the right place to be. So hang on for dear life. And don't let him eat you.

Reflaction—Your Resilience Plan

What doesn't kill you makes you stronger. There's a ton of truth packed in those words. But you can also make yourself stronger before the darkest day comes your way.

How? By developing your resilience plan. Parts of this process will be uncomfortable. If you're going to course correct, you have to be honest about your effort and results. If your financial health isn't where it should be, you have to take accountability and then action. If you've made excuses for why your physical health is poor, you have to put those excuses to death. Same for your social health and any other area you've identified for yourself.

A good place to start is by reflecting on your darkest days thus far. Write down those events—confront them. What actions did you take that helped? Which ones didn't help? What do you wish had been different? Who was there to help you?

CHAPTER 9: **OVERCOMING THE DARKEST DAYS**

With these questions, you can start to identify what your resilience plan needs to look like to be ready for the next darkest day. By identifying your weak spots, you may even prevent the type of darkest day that results from your own actions. At the very least, you'll be better equipped for the next one that comes along by circumstance.

On that note, remember that only the paranoid survive, so be a little paranoid for a moment.

Write out some potential threats to your success. If you work for a company, then the market could be a threat. It only takes a downturn or bad quarterly report for many companies to start slashing jobs. How vulnerable does that make you? Are you prepared for the worst?

Do you have a support network established outside of your colleagues at work? Have you separated your sense of self-worth from your profession? Have you defined your purpose and values to serve as your pivot point?

The resources you identify will serve you well when you come to your next juncture. You only have those three paths—dropping out, returning to status quo, or digging deeper. The beauty of digging deeper is that you not only discover your direction, but you discover the most valuable parts of who you are. The darkest days transform into a beam of light leading you to your truest, most authentic identity.

As you work through each piece of your resilience plan, you'll be making small course corrections that add up to a huge difference in your direction. Even if those corrections end up adjusting your destination somewhat, you'll move closer to where you're meant to be. For underdogs, the darkest days aren't the impediments to success—they become the accelerators.

AVENUE OF APPROACH 4

BUILD CREDIBILITY

CHAPTER 10

Establishing Professional Credibility

Credibility is a leader's currency. With it, he or she is solvent; without it, he or she is bankrupt.
—JOHN C. MAXWELL, BESTSELLING AUTHOR AND LEADERSHIP COACH

Like any good journalist, Tom Callahan had a penchant for sniffing out BS, a skill he had honed during his service in the Marine Corps. During the Greater Milwaukee Open in August of 1996, he met Earl Woods, the father of Tiger Woods. It's not unusual for parents to show pride in their children, but Tom was taken aback by Earl's consistent claims that his son would become the most famous golfer in the world. After all, Tiger was still a newcomer and two months away from his first PGA Tour victory.

Tom decided to play along and asked Earl where the name Tiger had come from. Earl explained it was actually a nickname given in honor of Lt. Colonel Nguyen "Tiger" Phong, a South Vietnamese officer who had become his best friend during the war. Earl went on to say he had served two tours in Vietnam as a Green Beret, though he couldn't remember the exact years—a detail that Tom found unbelievable.

Earl continued, explaining how he had always wanted to find out what happened to Tiger Phong after the war. And since he was convinced his son would go on to be world famous, Earl nicknamed him Tiger in the hopes that Tiger Phong would hear about him and reconnect.

Tom later wrote, "I took him for a complete blowhard … everything about Earl Woods was far-fetched."[13] So he decided to investigate Earl's claim about Tiger Phong and expose the BS. But as Tom investigated, more proof came to light that Earl had been telling the truth.

In the end, Tom's investigative trip to Vietnam revealed that there had indeed been a Colonel Tiger Phong, though he was now long gone. In fact, he had died after just six months of captivity in a prison/reeducation camp not far from the one where my own father was kept.[14]

Earl's story gained credibility when Tom found the proof. And Tiger, of course, proved his own credibility on the course by racking up win after win. No one watching him could doubt they were seeing the burgeoning career of an all-time great. Call it prophecy or preparation (or both), Earl Woods's words about his son being world famous came true.

Credibility is only developed one way—through action. You cannot think or talk your way to credibility. People must be able to see the proof.

Yet this is a major gap for many driven individuals. They believe they are ready for the next step—the management job, the depart-

---

[13] Tom Callahan, "In Search of Tiger Phong," GolfDigest.com, May 6, 2020, https://www.golfdigest.com/story/tiger-phong-gd199710.

[14] Tom Callahan, "In Search of Tiger Phong."

CHAPTER 10: **ESTABLISHING PROFESSIONAL CREDIBILITY**

mental move, the startup venture—and yet they have not put in the work to establish their credibility through actions.

That's exactly what I faced when transitioning from the Marines to pharmaceutical sales. The seasoned reps wanted to know who this upstart Marine was stepping into their territory. I had to prove myself before I could be accepted as part of the club. But once I established credibility through consistent sales numbers and medical knowledge, they began to take me seriously.

The same could be said when I left sales to start a company. I'd never raised a dollar from an investor, never been a CEO, but I could provide proof through market research, showing a solid business plan. Plus, I filled my team with individuals who could fill my own credibility gaps—and with a little Vietnamese chutzpah. That's how I turned twenty PowerPoint slides into $5 million twenty-five years ago.

But how do you start filling the credibility gap? What are the right approaches for gaining the experience you need to be taken seriously?

The Experience Problem

Experience can be a chicken-egg problem. On the one hand, companies want to hire people with experience—but you need to get hired to gain the experience.

When possible, you can solve the experience problem by being ready when your number is called. In wartime, you want to know the people next to you have combat experience. The problem we had in 1991 was the long gap between Vietnam and the Gulf War. In fact, the only person in our squadron with any combat experience whatsoever was our CO.

Every one of us flying on that first mission into Kuwait was experiencing combat for the first time. We were all equals in that regard.

But when we came back, we had instant credibility that we wore on our uniforms in the form of ribbons and awards. Suddenly, I wasn't a newbie anymore, but one of the seniors—a combat veteran.

You never know when the opportunity will come, so be prepared by doing the extra. Dak Prescott had played two seasons of college ball for Mississippi State University when he was drafted by the Dallas Cowboys in the fourth round of the 2016 NFL draft. At the time, Tony Romo was quarterback and had no intentions of retiring.

But then Romo was injured in the preseason. Suddenly, the rookie Prescott found himself as QB for "America's Team." The unusual circumstances led to Prescott being the first rookie quarterback in the Cowboys' history to start all sixteen games of the regular season.

Though he had zero professional experience, he quickly gained credibility as he led the team to a 13–3 record, including winning the NFC East title and selection to the Pro Bowl. Fast forward to 2024, Prescott became the highest-paid quarterback in the NFL—because he's earned the credentials. (However, he has yet to reach the Super Bowl—so there is still room to grow his credibility further.)

When you have a credibility gap—like Prescott did—you have to show results fast. It's not going to happen by accident. Recognize you have a steep learning curve ahead of you, and then do whatever you need to do to fill it.

No one is going to hand you the experience. You have to go out and claim it. If you're waiting to gain experience until you have the position, then you're too late. Ideally, you want to gain experience that is both relevant now and for the future.

For instance, when I started going through Toastmasters, I was still working for Genentech. While other reps were off having fun after hours, I was working my way through the training. Certainly, I knew the skills I was learning would help me be a better salesperson at the time, but I knew that if I was serious about running a startup someday, I'd need to improve my pitching skills to convince investors.

There's no law against gaining skills whenever you want them. Look ahead at the experience you're lacking and then take the actions to acquire them. Read a book. Take a course. Take a part-time position. You won't have return on investment (ROI) right away, so think of everything you do as an investment in yourself. The more you put in, the more it compounds into credibility.

Remember, no one is born with a PhD. No one just wakes up as an expert. Experience is gained as a result of your efforts to learn, prepare, and then take action.

When you don't have much experience yet, then use the experience you *do* have to compensate. Depending on your age, you might remember the 1980s classic show *MacGyver*. In each episode, the infinitely resourceful MacGyver utilized whatever objects he had available to stop the bad guys or escape whatever scrape he was in.

In the very first episode, he used string, a box of matches, and a cord to put together a timed machine-gun rig. In a later episode, he used a rubber glove, a hanging light bulb, and a gas line to create a small explosive so he could escape the villain. And in a particularly famous episode, he used a fallen satellite, some duct tape, and an old parachute to create a hang glider.

As ridiculous as these scenarios may be, they teach an important business lesson: when you're lean and scrappy, you've got to MacGyver a way forward. In MacGyver's underdog nation, nothing is wasted. None of your own experiences are wasted if you see them as resources for confidence and credibility.

The Power of Networking

What you know is important. But who you know is invaluable. When you have a credibility gap, then one of the best solutions is to borrow someone else's credibility. No matter where you are in your career, you'll find benefits from utilizing the credibility of others to support you. Consider what happens when you provide a potential employer with your list of references. Or perhaps a colleague has offered guidance as you advanced in your particular career.

But networking is just as important as you climb the ladder.

Whenever you pitch to an investor, rarely do they only care about the product and the market research. Yes, those are important, but they aren't everything. They also want to know the following:

- Who is on your team (CFO, COO, sales/marketing, product design, etc.)?

- Who are you already partnered with (sponsors, distribution partners, suppliers)?

- Who are you already serving (customers/clientele)?

You might be the face of the company, but these three *whos* are huge credibility boosts—assuming you have the right people. But how do you expect to find those team members and business partners if you're not developing your network?

Putting my full efforts into the aide-de-camp role during my last year of active duty was the best action I took. I came out of the service with a CRM's worth of contacts who knew my reputation as a Marine and whom I was able to call upon in the future.

And remember how I was the only sales rep at Astra/Merck willing to network with the CEO Wayne Yetter? Connecting with

CHAPTER 10: ESTABLISHING PROFESSIONAL CREDIBILITY

him over our shared military experience laid the stage for him to later become my most trusted board member.

In today's digital world, it's never been easier—or more important—to network. Your online profile isn't just a digital résumé for people to stumble across—it's your strategic credibility builder. Let's not pretend any of us can accurately predict the future. The connection you make today could be your most valuable collaborator tomorrow—or next year—or next decade.

As much as people like to complain about social media, it's much better than the old system of submitting a piece of paper with only your name and a few bullet points. Now people have the opportunity to see you in action, to hear about your values and thoughts. If they don't align with what you're doing, they'll move on and you've lost nothing. If they align and reach out, then you've gained influence and credibility.

You don't need a million followers to gain credibility either. You simply need intentional connection. Your next job, your next company, your next big deal could be one connection away. Just one.

In any profession, you're going to discover you have gaps. No one can know everything. And you can't DIY everything, either because you lack the time or talent. You'll need experts who can lend you their credibility and insights to lift you up.

These lessons are all part of CEO 101, but you don't need to be a CEO to apply them to your situation. If you're burned out where you are, you're not going to have the kindling to reignite yourself. You'll need to find it elsewhere.

"But Quang, I'm an introvert." No problem. You're in good company: Gandhi, Eleanor Roosevelt, Martin Luther King Jr., Nelson Mandela, and Barack Obama. All of them excelled with connecting because they spoke from a place of humble confidence.

In fact, you'll be a better networker if you approach the task with humble confidence. If you go in guns blazing, people will assume you just want to sell them on something, and they'll put up a wall.

Whenever I give a presentation, my focus is on being factual and entertaining—people get bored easily these days. The facts keep me humble and confident. The focus is on the business case for the investment. You can do the same. When people ask what you do, shine the light on the problem you solve for people, the wins that others have experienced, or how great your team is. Make your case relatable.

It's a modern myth that you have to be the high-energy, super-charismatic visionary CEO to connect with people. Nor do you have to be a comedian to be funny and engaging.

Another myth of modern networking is that it's about quantity, but the truth is that it's about quality. Having ten million followers is one metric for credibility, but so is having one follower who invests five million in your company. Networking at its most powerful is a one-to-one connection, not one-to-one million.

The best part of networking is that so much of it is in *your* control. When I first moved into pharmaceutical sales, I was given the territory of western Los Angeles, which represented around three hundred prescribers I could call upon. If I was going to scale, I'd have to find ways to grow that number.

Whenever I could, I took on extra assignments. If the chance came up to attend a convention and sit at an informational booth for the company, I raised my hand. Many of the other reps hated these assignments because they saw them as time away from their dependable customers. I saw them as a chance to grow my network, be on the front lines like in the Marines. Always go where the action is.

Same thing within the company. If there was a rewards trip available for sales reps or a reception hosted by the VPs, I made sure

CHAPTER 10: **ESTABLISHING PROFESSIONAL CREDIBILITY**

to be there. That's why I met Wayne within my first three months at Astra/Merck.

Read up on people's profiles—what are their hobbies or interests? Find the common ground and you'll automatically have a talking point you can connect over. Maybe it's a sport like golf, or you both have kids, or you both read the same type of books. You can always find a way to connect with others. And when you do, you first earn connection, then rapport, then credibility.

Criticism and Conflict

Not everyone is going to believe in you. That's good. When people don't believe in you, your inner underdog thrives. When you're approached with skepticism, you can use it to grow your confidence. And criticism, when filtered correctly, helps you close your credibility gaps. Don't confuse critics with haters. Critics care; haters just whine.

The main criticism you'll face in life is any lack of firsthand experience you may have. When that happens, you highlight your strengths. Use the power of storytelling to overcome the objections.

When I was a brand-new CEO facing investors for the first time with MyDrugRep.com, some of them asked me, "How do we know you can do this?"

Fair question. Even though I had no experience in the world of startups, I was able to draw on my previous wins:

"I've operated under the pressure of combat on a real front line, when the outcome was life or death. Despite my lack of experience in sales, I became the top pharmaceutical rep. That's how I identified the inefficiencies in the drug rep process and recognized we can use the internet to overcome those inefficiencies."

But what about when the criticism feels unfair? When I started working in pharmaceutical sales, the question that came up the most was this: "Well, if you wanted to get into the private sector all along, then why did you even go into the military? Why not start in pharma sales? Wouldn't you be further along in your career now?"

When this criticism happens, you've got to go back to your personal values. Whenever I faced these comments, I would remind myself *I needed to serve my country. I wanted to be a pilot like my father. I had limited time to make that happen.*

Many veterans leaving the service face anti-veteran bias within the private sector. The assumptions go like this: "They only know how to take orders, not be creative. They don't have P&L experience; they don't know marketing." These biases taught me to quickly develop a filter for criticism.

If the individual coming with the criticism has some knowledge of the problem and circumstances, then I should listen. If they are only making assumptions, then the criticism can be discounted.

The other filter I use for criticism is to remind myself *I'm human. I'm not perfect.*

We all make mistakes, so when criticism comes along, assess whether there is a gap you haven't filled yet. Is there some area where you need to improve more than others? This type of criticism is valuable because it helps you find those blind spots and address them faster. When you close that gap, you only become more credible.

Likewise, no one can perfectly avoid all conflict. Nor should you. Conflict serves to make you stronger.

When you're surrounding yourself with smart people, there may come a point where they believe they can do your job better than you. And guess what? You *want* that to happen.

CHAPTER 10: **ESTABLISHING PROFESSIONAL CREDIBILITY**

Everyone is replaceable, including the CEO. You want people who know the business so well that if something happens to you, they could step in and do your job—maybe even better than you. You need to have people who are willing to fight for the good of the business, who can communicate and pitch the story as well as you do.

Conflict needs to exist in a balance. Too little and you're in an environment of "yes" people where complacency will creep in. Too much conflict and you're in a toxic environment built on fear and politicking. But the right amount of conflict helps expose the gaps and develop both your credibility and the company's credibility.

The filter with conflict is a simple question: What battles are worth fighting?

Once again, you go back to your values to choose which battles to fight. Look at the big picture, especially when you're in conflict with one other person. Ask yourself, "Am I better off having this person on the team? Or should we part over this particular issue?" Or another key question: "Do they provide answers or just ask questions and criticize?"

Maybe you have conflict with them, but they are moving the business forward. Maybe the conflict is helping expose the gaps. If so, then it's better to put aside your ego and not get bogged down in the battle. If you see they are helping at a higher level, then forgive and move on. Because you also gain credibility and trust from others when they see you don't have to fight over every little issue.

Reflaction—Fake It 'til You Make It

In the military, we all wanted to be the helicopter aircraft commander, not the copilot. But moving over to the captain's chair meant you had to be cleared by the captain. Ultimately, it was their decision, and you had to prove you knew how to lead, complete the mission, and operate safely. You had to envision yourself doing those actions before they actually happened.

To me, this type of envisioning exercise is the epitome of the "fake it 'til you make it strategy." You have to approach the situation as if you've done it a thousand times, even when it's the first time.

Some people won't like this advice. Certainly, there are life-and-death situations in which you should not fake it. Those are the times to rely on someone else's expertise and credentials. But that's not what I'm talking about here.

The "fake it 'til you make it" approach has validity in terms of envisioning the success you want. If you wait to have confidence and credibility for when you've made it, then the unfortunate reality is you *never* will make it. *Just do it.*

Remember when we entered the pitch competition against the likes of Harvard, Yale, Stanford, and the London School of Economics? Our UC Irvine team was the definition of underdog in that competition, which is part of why my number two thought we were wasting our time. He wasn't being a Debbie Downer, just a strategic realist. He recognized the uphill battle of being an untested startup with a brand-new CEO who had never raised capital before.

We couldn't be confident in the outcome yet, but I had confidence in the idea. I had to leverage that mental confidence to fake the external confidence I needed for a great presentation. And while it was true I'd never raised funding for a startup before, my experience as a pharmaceutical rep meant I knew what it was like to raise millions in capital through sales. My thousands of conversations with doctors (called *detailing*) offered proof that a better system could be developed.

CHAPTER 10: **ESTABLISHING PROFESSIONAL CREDIBILITY**

So the first step in this reflection is to make a list of all your transferable skills. What are the experiences and abilities you have today that can transfer over into the role you want?

For instance, name a single job where writing isn't a valuable skill. Even CEOs need to have enough writing abilities to recognize good copy in a press release that's going to have their name on it. The same could be said with other forms of communication, interpersonal skills, organizational skills, basic accounting, and so on.

Let's say you're in sales now—you have to become a master of your job. You have to know your product, your competitors, the client's needs, and the market trends backward and forward. That knowledge and experience can be leveraged into confidence so you can fake it 'til you make it. All those experiences are transferable skills.

The next step is to then identify the gaps between where you are and where you want to be. If you're still lower on the ladder, or in middle management, then your approach should be to find out what you need to learn to do your boss's job. If their seat was vacated tomorrow, would you have the skill set and confidence to take it over?

If you can't answer yes, then there is a credibility and knowledge gap you have to fill. To make it, you'll have to fake it. That is, you'll have to reverse engineer the skills needed to take over your boss's job—or whoever else's job it is you want.

Faking it 'til you make it is closely related to loving what you do until you can do what you love. Even if you don't love everything you do, give it your all so you can identify those knowledge gaps you need to fill.

Being the best salesperson in the company gave me the credibility and confidence I needed when I made the jump to entrepreneurship. It provided me with a laundry list of transferable skills.

So make sure you're documenting your achievements along the way—awards, recognition, dollar amounts of sales, certifications—anything that will help you become more credible. You'll reshape your identity into the picture of success you envisioned. You'll no longer only be credible—you'll be *incredible*.

CHAPTER 11

Navigating Your Identity

We know what we are, but not what we may be.
—WILLIAM SHAKESPEARE, *HAMLET*

You might expect a chapter on identity to come earlier on in a book like this, especially given how common discussions around identity have been in the past few years. A recurring problem I see with discussions around identity, however, is the notion that identity is fixed.

Not at all. Identity can be fluid.

When we fled Vietnam, our identity changed—totally outside of our control. We went from free citizens to displaced refugees. But some aspects of our identity were within our control. Mom chose not to anglicize our names because our names were connected with our homeland.

Later on, I had the chance to choose my professional identities. I chose to become a US Marine. (Not a John Wayne but a real Marine like Fred Smith of FedEx.) I chose to become a salesperson. I chose to become an entrepreneur. I chose to take risks and lead as a CEO.

And then there are the personal identities we adopt. When I got married, I adopted the identity of husband. When my daughter was born, I became Dad. When I got divorced, my identity reverted back to being single. I get to choose the identity of friend and who I share it with.

Much of life finds you navigating between identities, and it's not uncommon that you reach a crossroads where two identities come into conflict with one another—and you have a choice to make. You have an internal civil war over who you are going to be.

Most people passively take whatever identity is put upon them by their circumstances, heritage, veteran status, or socioeconomic status. Underdogs fight for their identity.

The Vietnam War has often been framed in the US as being between the Democratic West and the Communist East. But for those of us who lived there, it was a civil war of North against South. However, this North versus South aspect is where the similarities between our civil war and the American Civil War end.

During the American Civil War, the US had around 31.5 million residents. During the Vietnam War, Vietnam had around 38 million, with a slightly higher population in the North. It's estimated that over 600,000 American soldiers died in the Civil War—more than in any other US conflict.[15] When accounting for Vietnamese deaths on both sides, the number is staggering—over 1.25 million.[16]

Every civil war in history ultimately comes down to a battle over national identity. Or if not a battle, it can feel like walking a tightrope. While my family was assimilating into American culture, there was a

---

[15] American Battlefield Trust, "Civil War Casualties," Battlefields.org, November 16, 2012, updated September 15, 2023, https://www.battlefields.org/learn/articles/civil-war-casualties.

[16] R. H. Spector, "Vietnam War," *Encyclopedia Britannica, October 27, 2024*, https://www.britannica.com/event/Vietnam-War.

fine balance of being "American enough" that people wouldn't yell at us to learn English but not so American that our fellow Vietnamese immigrants would call us "bananas" (that is, yellow on the outside, white on the inside). More than once, I was told, "Your Vietnamese is not good. You're too busy speaking English."

It was a demanding position to be in, straddling identities in America.

Throughout your life, you'll also straddle identities. You're going to find yourself in various cultural contexts where a certain identity is going to be impressed upon you. It might sound like the following:

Professional: "When you walk outside these walls, you represent the company. That's why we'll be monitoring your social media …"

Personal: "Why can't you be more like your cousin? Maybe then you'd be happy."

Veteran: "I thought you were in the Marines. You're not so tough."

Ultimately, the way of the underdog is to become comfortably anchored in your own personal identity. True authenticity is having the confidence to be yourself no matter where you are.

If you allow others to shape your identity, then you also allow them and the environment to define success for you. But no one else can tell you who you are—or who you will be. That's your journey. And you get to shape it through your effort and results.

The more you are able to navigate your identity on your terms, the less likely you'll experience an identity civil war within yourself. You'll be more centered, more authentic, and more capable of achieving the success you've envisioned for yourself.

Become Known for Your Effort and Results

When you join a new organization, you want to be there. You're excited about the new opportunity, the new pay, maybe even the prestige of a better title. You're eager to showcase what you're bringing to the table—but you also end up assimilating into the new work culture.

Where people go awry with their workplace identity is allowing the work culture to shape what they are known for rather than being known for their effort and results. They become no more than the title on their nameplate, which is a dangerous place to be.

The good news is that the American corporate culture is less rigid than it was thirty years ago. While some environments are not as flexible, there is more freedom to bring your personal life into the workplace than in days past. Pets and kids popping in for Zoom-call cameos are not only accepted but expected. Discussions around hobbies, beliefs, and other pursuits are now encouraged for building common ground rather than immediately dismissed as a breeding ground for conflict.

With this freedom, you have an opportunity to be known not only for your extracurriculars but for the extra value you're providing to the workplace. You get to choose what accomplishments you want to highlight as part of your corporate identity.

For instance, consider the common interview question "What did you do at Company X?"

Many people will reply, "Well, we were part of the Initiative Y and Project Z that was so successful."

See the problem here? It seems so innocent at first, but the problem is the word *we*.

Whenever I hear an answer with the word *we,* I like to redirect by asking, "Yes, but what did *you* do there? What was your contribution to Initiative Y and Project Z?"

This isn't an accusation. It's an invitation for them to highlight their own contributions! *We* is indicative that you're not defining your own professional identity. You're choosing to be known by a collective effort and result rather than being specific. But the real power is in the specificity. For example, nearly everyone I know from Pfizer claimed that they took part in the launch of Viagra. Hardly!

You're better off answering, "I was the lead copywriter during the Initiative Y campaign, so I managed all of our social media channels during the initial product launch."

By highlighting your specific effort and results, you've made your identity much more distinct than taking credit for the collective accomplishment. Even if your only job was to go on the coffee run and order supplies, it speaks to your dedication to be a resource for others. I would much rather hire the person with that profile than the person who takes credit for someone else's work.

Titles should never form the core of your professional identity because they can be misleading. A title's meaning can vary wildly from company to company. The director of events at one business might be the lead for all corporate events, like product launches and conferences. But at another organization, they might be a glorified keeper of the company's social calendar.

Align Your Values to Your Actions

In the last chapter, we touched on the idea of using your values as a filter with criticism. But your values should also be the guidepost for your actions, that is, your efforts. Your values give you a target to aim for. They make the mission simple.

When I was still piloting, my favorite CO put it this way: "Your job isn't about wearing a nice dress-blue uniform, saying 'Oorah,' or any of that other crap. Your mission is to get into the effing right landing zone on time. Don't make it more complicated. Everything you do in our squadron is to make sure you're in that damn landing zone to pick up Marines on time. In zone, on time."

His description cut through the stress and anxiety that could come along with flying a mission. And that's what core values do—they narrow your scope so you can see the landing zone more clearly.

Toward the tail end of my time with the general, I knew I would have great recommendations. The question was what job would best align with my values.

One of the resources available to junior military officers (JMOs) transferring out of the service were JMO recruiters. Their job was to help us find suitable professional work opportunities. The problem was that they rarely wanted to do placements for people over the age of thirty. At the time, there was a pervading sense that "you can't teach an old dog new tricks."

We were sent out on a series of interviews, attended a conference, and were even flown out to meet with various big companies. For the most part, the hiring managers I met with were looking for sharp young officers who were hungry for success. They were also looking for people in three main functional areas: operations, finance, and sales. All of these are areas you can be trained for.

During the process, I gravitated toward sales because I felt like it was built on many of the same values that had inspired me to be a pilot. It required reliability, discipline, and a keen knowledge of

CHAPTER 11: **NAVIGATING YOUR IDENTITY**

standard operating procedures. Once I settled on the sales function, I had several offers come my way.

One of the most appealing offers was for a brand manager position at a major consumer goods company. I fit the personality profile as well as anyone could, and the work sounded interesting. Unfortunately, the role would have required me to move to the Midwest. But with so much of my support system in SoCal, the geography was a deal-breaker. Middle America was outside my landing zone, which made the opportunity simpler to turn down.

The same value played a role in a go/no-go decision later on when I was offered a position in medical equipment sales with GE. This was at the pinnacle of medical equipment sales, so the pay would have been tremendous. But when I asked about where I would work, they explained, "Well, you get the next territory available, wherever that is." Once again, my value for geography made the decision simpler, so I turned it down.

Looking back, I'm glad I did because otherwise, I would have missed out on taking actions more closely aligned with my values. Because I stayed in SoCal longer, the opportunity at Genentech opened up for me to move into some breakthrough oncology drugs. These drugs were "smart bomb" monoclonal antibodies that could target cancerous cells while leaving the healthy cells alone.

While I had given my all to my other jobs, finally this was the opportunity where I could both be successful and make a real difference. Not that drugs like Prilosec weren't making a difference for people. But this was definitely more aligned with the mark I wanted to leave on the world, especially as I looked forward to one day starting my own company. The groundwork for Cadrenal and tecarfarin was being laid even then.

When your values form your compass, it will save you from getting lost in the smoke. Money is nice, but it will blind you if you don't know your bearings. If you're even a percent off from where you need to go, then who knows where you'll end up? And you may run out of gas before you can course correct. If you don't reach the landing zone on time, then the mission is a failure. Or if you reach the wrong landing zone, well, you and your crew may be in danger—along with the Marines who are depending on you.

To begin aligning your values with your actions, practice the following:

1. Right or wrong, make a decision. (Use go/no-go decision-making.)
2. Be in zone, on time. (Simplify the mission.)
3. Take action in the objective area. Make it count. (Take yourself to the ER. Right effort, right results.)

On this last one, it's all about putting your training and resources to work. When I was in sales, we were well trained for the job, but I noticed some reps never made use of their training or the tools they were given. In the Marines, all your training matters. When you get into that landing zone and you're taking fire, or the other helicopter is shot down, or your wingman goes down, your survival depends on your training. It all matters.

In sales, it wasn't so life and death, of course. But the way this approach translated in sales was that I had to see the right doctor, deliver the right message, and do so with the right frequency. Failing to take these actions in the objective area would mean failing to live up to my values and failing to fulfill the mission.

CHAPTER 11: **NAVIGATING YOUR IDENTITY**

Shaping Your Future Identity

Think for a second about your definition of success. Envision your future self. What is the gap between your identity now and this future identity?

Don't worry so much about how large the gap might be. Why not? Because you are going to bridge that gap with your effort and results. However, bridging the gap will be impossible if you're continually looking back.

For eight years, my identity had been tied to the Marine Corps. And for the first twelve to eighteen months I was in sales, I carried much of that identity with me into pharma sales. I was used to higher standards of conduct, discipline, and work ethic than what I was seeing. For example, it drove me nuts that every meeting started late.

Eventually, I made comments that isolated me from my peers. Statements like "You know, in the Marines, if you're not five minutes early, then you're late." My remarks were what led to the snide retorts of "Well, if you liked it so much, then why don't you go back?"

In trying to bridge my credibility gap, I was clinging to my glory days. I simply wasn't comfortable with my new identity yet. And shaping a new identity as a top salesperson would be impossible if I didn't adjust my effort and results. By taking myself to the ER, I realized it was imperative to cut down on the Marine chatter and double down on sales performance.

You can't build your future without proving yourself in the present. And you can't prove yourself in the present by only relying on the past. I realized it didn't matter if everyone else was late to a meeting—the fact that I was early made me stand out.

And later on when I became the CEO I had envisioned for myself, I kept my personal value of punctuality, but I chose not to get upset at people who were late. It wasn't a battle worth fighting.

But I always started meetings on time out of respect for the people who were punctual.

Reshaping your identity doesn't mean you eradicate who you were. Rather, your old identity becomes the building blocks for who you need to be now *and* in the future. So much of what I learned about leadership came straight from the Marine Corps. Simon Sinek may have written the book *Leaders Eat Last*, but I'd already learned that value in the Marines, where officers *always* ate last.

But in looking to the future, you also have to modulate from who you've been. As a kid, I was always a fast player in sports, mostly from impatience. In adulthood, I learned the hard way that it's rarely the first mover who wins but the one who makes the first *right* move. During my first marathon, I sprinted out of the gate, ran out of steam, hit a wall, and had to walk the last few miles. A few years later, I cut my time by nearly eighty minutes.

Likewise, my entire career in entrepreneurship, I've struggled with patience. And believe me, when you're in drug development—with all the FDA red tape—you better learn to be patient.

So while the lesson of "leaders eat last" from the Marines helped me shape my future identity as a CEO, my impatience was a detriment. By my second marathon, I had learned to pace myself and dropped forty minutes off my time. My identity as a marathon runner taught me a lesson I could bring over to the business world—to foster the patience to finish the race well. And that meant run at a pace, operate at a pace so that the entire team can finish and not burn out.

Are there matters that need to get done with more urgency? Yes. But not everything has to be done right away. Nor can you expect everyone else—like the FDA—to operate on your personal timeline.

You can take the best parts of your past to shape your future. And you can leave the unhelpful parts out. By removing the efforts that don't get you the results you need, you create room for more of the efforts you *should* be taking.

Start by taking a fresh look at your résumé or bio. Often, people have a tendency to put every single accomplishment and position on the page. But what pieces of your past do you need to actually highlight as part of your new identity? Do you still want to be seen as the burger flipper? If not, then drop it from the résumé. And make sure you leave space on the page for who you want to become. The right employer will see the potential on the page.

This exercise will help you pinpoint the parts of your past identities that can become building blocks for your future identity. But it will also help you see which parts to edit out.

All the more reason to align your identity with your effort and results, not with your title. Titles are given, but your results are earned. Results will win you far more credibility as you evolve into your future self.

Reflaction—Find Your Boat

When I was serving in the Persian Gulf on my second deployment, we took off from amphibious ships. When taking off, we never said "fly off the carrier." We'd say "fly off the boat."

If it was a night mission we were flying, hovering over the darkness of the sea, we would then have to *find* the boat. The seas were always changing, unpredictable. But the boat was steady, our source of constancy. We always remembered its heading, its plan of intended movement (or PIM).

To create constancy in your self-awareness, you must find balance. You need to find your boat for when the seas grow rough and the wind howls. When you've had a long, tough day, or a bad month, or a dismal quarter, you can go back to the boat, knowing that eventually, the tide will recede and the floods will subside.

Like the ebb and flow of the tide, your identity is fluid, but your boat represents the part of your identity that gives you direction, no matter your job title. Your core identity can become your strong home base, your constant in a sea of doubts. For many people, the boat is their family, their faith, their friends, a hobby, or a significant other.

Think back to your support system. Who are the people around you whom you can depend on? The people you can call for counsel and help?

Consider the activities that keep you grounded. What helps you stay financially, emotionally, and physically healthy? What efforts allow you to diffuse stress and stay positive? Who are you around when you're doing these activities?

Reflect on the values that help you make decisions and take actions. What are your deal-breakers? What does "in zone, on time" look like for you? Have you defined the right actions, in the right place, at the right time?

One area where the analogy differs from my Marine experience is that you're not only landing on the boat for respite—you're also the captain. When you find your boat, you use it to navigate your identity on the journey to success.

You'll find many forces trying to push or pull you to the identities they want. Sometimes they will be external, sometimes internal. Some are critics; some are haters. Some will respect you; others will envy you. Some will include you; others will keep you out of their circle. All of them push you toward the brink of an identity civil war. Your inner underdog can rise to the challenge.

Let your inner underdog recognize that changes and challenges are not your enemy—they help define your purpose. Just like with

CHAPTER 11: **NAVIGATING YOUR IDENTITY**

an aircraft carrier, the sea rises and falls, storms come and go, but without the waves, the ship serves no purpose. Despite the changes and challenges of the world, you must develop constancy in your self-awareness.

CHAPTER 12

Aligning Personal Purpose and Company Mission

Human beings need to have a purpose, not just missions and goals.
—GENERAL COLIN POWELL

While I was working on this book, Hurricane Helene struck the Southeast, creating devastation for millions. The day after the storm hit, David Jones, a sixty-four-year-old business coach, ended up traveling the distance of a marathon through hurricane debris—in the dark and mostly by foot.

It was a dangerous decision. Foolish even. But he had a reason why.

His daughter was getting married at 11:00 a.m. the next morning, and he was determined to walk her down the aisle.

When the storm hit on September 27, 2024, he was at his home in Boiling Springs, South Carolina. His daughter was to be married in Johnson City, Tennessee—a drive that normally took around two hours.

After the storm passed, he set out in his Ford Explorer and made it all the way across the state line. But at around 2:00 a.m., he came to a line of cars and trucks stopped on the interstate. Law enforcement officers had shut down the highway, telling drivers they had to turn around. When David told officers he had to get through, they said, "You can't. The bridges are out. Nobody can get through."

David had a house in Johnson City, so he knew the area. Plus, he'd run marathons and figured he could cover the remaining twenty-seven miles in nine hours. Despite the warnings of the police officers, he embraced his underdog spirit, parked his vehicle, grabbed some supplies, including a windbreaker and a reflector, and struck out on foot.

Along the way, he saw the extent of devastation—fallen trees, power out, no lights, entire sections of road washed out. Multiple state troopers tried to stop him from moving forward. "My daughter's getting married at eleven o'clock," he said, like a mantra. "I'm going to be there to walk her down the aisle."[17]

When he saw a backhoe clearing the road, surrounded by seven-foot-high piles of debris, he decided to try to go ahead of it—and fell straight down into "mud that was like quicksand."[18]

He finally managed to get his right leg free but lost his shoe and had to dig it out. At one point, his phone went dead until a trooper found him and gave him a short ride into downtown Erwin, Tennessee. But David was then back on foot, and time was not in his favor. He knew he might have to settle for a backup plan—watch his daughter's wedding over Zoom.

Still, he was going to give everything he had and kept walking. A truck pulled over, and the driver offered him a ride. I don't know about you, but I'm not sure I would hitchhike in rural Tennessee

---

[17] Wendy Grossman Kantor, "Determined Dad Treks Nearly 30 Miles Through Hurricane Debris to Be at Daughter's Wedding," People, September 30, 2024, https://people.com/dad-walks-nearly-30-miles-through-hurricane-debris-for-daughters-wedding-exclusive-8720636.

[18] Wendy Kantor, "Determined Dad."

CHAPTER 12: **ALIGNING PERSONAL PURPOSE AND COMPANY MISSION**

in the wake of a hurricane. But David was determined and took his chances. Turns out the driver was actually an old coworker from decades before.

Coincidence? Or destiny?

His old coworker drove him the last eight miles to his house in Johnson City, where David was able to wash up, change into a spare suit, and make it to the wedding by 11:00 a.m. just like he had envisioned—and walked his daughter down the aisle. For a wedding gift, he presented the happy couple with the reflector he had carried on the journey—a reminder of just how far he was willing to go for her.

Without David's purpose, the story of a sixty-four-year-old man trudging through hurricane debris makes no sense. But his purpose made all the difference. And yet, in an interview with *People* magazine, he simply stated, "I did what any dad would do."[19]

Since I'm a fellow marathoner and girl dad, David's story resonates with me deeply. His marathon training prepared him for this moment. When his number was called, he was ready. His choice to center purpose transformed the coincidence of a deadly hurricane into destiny.

Purpose is the ultimate game changer for the underdog. When I went into the Marines, it was from a place of purpose, because the system was not in my favor. When I transitioned from Astra/Merck to Genentech, it was because of purpose—both Genentech's pay structure and products were more aligned with my personal values. When we started Cadrenal to resurrect tecarfarin from the ashes of Espero, it was because of purpose.

Sometimes the moves you make will look crazy to other people, like you're walking through hurricane debris. It may even feel like that to you sometimes. But when you can align personal purpose with

---

19   Wendy Kantor, "Determined Dad."

company mission, then you wield the full power and potential of the underdog. It is the secret ingredient for long-term success.

THE SECRET INGREDIENT

For any goal to translate into success, the secret ingredient is purpose. And yet, this often appears to be the missing ingredient.

According to research, 62 percent of people never even make a New Year's resolution. Of the 38 percent who do make a New Year's resolution, 80 percent of those let their goals fall by the wayside before Valentine's Day. By the end of the year, only 9 percent of resolution makers can say they stuck with them.[20]

The numbers tell a story—that most people lack any kind of personal purpose driving their decisions.

I'm willing to bet that the reason over half of people don't even attempt a resolution is because of a false belief that if you don't set a goal, then you can't fail. No underdog thinks this way. And it's a defeatist way to live.

For the 91 percent of people who do make resolutions but fail to succeed, I have no doubt that there wasn't necessarily a failure in desire, but a failure to look at effort and results. Perhaps they didn't get the immediate results they wanted, so instead of adjusting their effort, they dropped out. Or perhaps they decided the result wasn't worth the effort and dropped out.

The stats show that if you make a New Year's resolution, you're already an underdog. The stats are against you. The Vegas odds are decidedly *not* in your favor.

---

20   Lark Allen, "New Year's Resolutions Statistics and Trends [2023]," Drive Research, September 13, 2023, https://www.driveresearch.com/market-research-company-blog/new-years-resolutions-statistics/#.

CHAPTER 12: **ALIGNING PERSONAL PURPOSE AND COMPANY MISSION**

Goals and success are not the same, but they *are* related. You cannot reach success without goals. Goals define your target landing zone and the time to land. They transform an intangible idea of success into a tangible plan.

To become part of the 9 percent of underdogs who succeed with their goals, you must have purpose. And if purpose is absent, ask yourself why you're even considering that specific goal. Could the goal in question actually be indicative of someone else defining success for you?

So much of this goes back to whether you can envision your success. Don't be a dreamer. Be a doer.

As a kid, I envisioned myself climbing into that cockpit. The dream vanished for ten years. But when I was introduced to the Marine Corps, I envisioned myself as an officer and never once considered that I wouldn't make it through Officer Candidates School. I saw my wings of gold already on me and followed up with actions.

Despite the failures I've encountered, I always envision success with any new venture. By zeroing in on the profiles of other successful people, I also zero in on the obstacles that could trip me up.

For instance, the one athletic area I always struggled in was swimming. But I knew that naval aviators have to be strong swimmers. So before training started, I climbed into the pool every day and practiced swimming on my own, putting in the effort to achieve the results I envisioned.

If you find there's a skill or area where you are deficient, do something about it early and often. Your success depends on it. Your credibility is at stake. When you have purpose as the secret ingredient, you don't see failure as an option. Instead you see roadblocks to overcome.

Through the eyes of purpose, see yourself as a success. Then you'll no longer be dreaming of the future you want; you'll be envisioning it. And if you're in a leadership position, don't talk about dreams—talk about vision. Vision is far more infectious when it comes to passing on the power of purpose.

Purpose Is a Choice

When purpose is discussed, it is often presented as if it is bestowed like a divine spark. In my experience, though, purpose is actually a choice. When companies create mission statements, the words never magically appear on the wall. The leadership team meets together, they brainstorm, they discuss with stakeholders, they define values and set vision, and then they develop the mission statement. Putting the mission statement up on the wall is simply the action that connects the choice to accountability.

Choosing a purpose takes real effort. Which means purpose can also generate real results.

A dangerous narrative I see lately within minority populations is the idea that the system is against you. While there is some truth to how systems have excluded people of color in a white world, this victim mentality forfeits the choice of purpose.

Ever since coming to America, I've had to live in "the White Man's World." As I mentioned before, I almost didn't join the Marines because of the racist overtones and anti-Asian mentality I saw due to the various wars in Asia. But time after time, I've made a conscious choice as a person of color to step into white spaces and to be the change maker. Changing the perception of my birth culture has been closely connected to both my identity and purpose.

CHAPTER 12: **ALIGNING PERSONAL PURPOSE AND COMPANY MISSION**

Therefore, the idea that you cannot bring your purpose into a challenging space is not only wrong, but it perpetuates the problem. You have to choose your purpose over the systemic challenges. Otherwise, nothing changes. Professional victims will continue to complain.

Systemic issues aside, nothing will derail the power of purpose more than the fear of the unknown when making a decision. So you must first recognize that there will always be unknowns in any decision. Waiting for 100 percent certainty will 100 percent lead you to failure and regret.

Years ago, I heard the late Colin Powell present on the topic of certainty in decision-making. He followed what he called the 40/70 rule regarding how much information is needed to speed up decision-making. He broke it down like this:

- If you have less than 40 percent of the information you need, then you're guessing, and therefore it's a bad decision.

- If you have more than 70 percent of the information you need, then you've waited too long. The decision is going to be made for you by circumstance or your competition.

In fact, we can even apply the 40/70 rule to the opening story of David Jones. He had at least 50 percent of the information necessary to make his decision about going on foot:

- He knew he had the physical stamina to walk the distance of twenty-seven miles.

- He knew the area well enough to have an idea of alternate routes, even with the bridges washed out.

- He knew that going on foot would enable him to bypass some obstructions that a vehicle couldn't handle.

- He knew he had nine hours to get to the wedding on time.
- He knew he had enough supplies to walk with reasonable safety.

Despite the unknowns of the obstacles he would face, there were enough knowns for him to reach past the 40 percent threshold in his mind. And then with the choice of purpose, he was able to decide quickly rather than waste another moment debating with himself or anyone else.

In my own work, I've had to use purpose to modulate my own tendencies for speed. In the dot-com era of MyDrugRep, everything was go-go-go. But with Cadrenal, I've had to take a more measured, patient approach because of the FDA requirements around orphan drug–designated trials. Whenever I become impatient, I go back to choosing purpose: *This drug will help save lives and disrupt the status quo of blood thinners.* When I choose purpose over impatience, it affects my decisions and my actions.

The underlying urgency to help people with rare cardiovascular conditions motivates me each day, but I daily make the choice of purpose to stay focused on the long game. Choosing purpose helps me remember it is a marathon, not a sprint. Choosing purpose helps me remain strategic so that we can pace ourselves to reach the finish line.

You have many choices in life, including who you work for and how much effort you put into that work. But the most important choice you can make with your work is to choose purpose. Otherwise, your efforts won't be there, the results won't be there, and success won't be there.

CHAPTER 12: **ALIGNING PERSONAL PURPOSE AND COMPANY MISSION**

Aligning Purpose with Company Mission

Unless it's your own company you started, you probably weren't at the table when the company's purpose and mission statement were chosen. However, you do have a choice to bring your purpose to work every day and find out how it overlaps with the purpose of the company.

Finding the overlap is what will drive you to love what you do until you can do what you love. Revisit the 20/80 rule from chapter 3 through the lens of purpose—can you find the 20 percent of the company's purpose that aligns with yours? If not, then you're definitely in the wrong place. Stop wasting your time and make the jump.

However, if you can find that 20 percent, then you can still make an impact on the existing corporate culture. Your efforts can still produce powerful results that move you along your journey to success.

But let's say it is your company. You may have injected your purpose and values into the mission, but misalignment is still possible. As you grow, misalignment is probably because you'll be bringing in new people with their own purposes and values which may conflict with the culture you've created.

Earlier I mentioned how one of my first entrepreneurial mistakes was when we made the second wave of hires at MyDrugRep. When we brought in a group of intelligent people with their Ivy League pedigrees, it created an unexpected culture clash I hadn't foreseen.

Since the beginning, I had established the company built on a value of go/no-go decision-making. Now I had a group of people arguing that we needed to slow down and do extensive modeling and research and quantitative analysis.

Finally, I had to put my foot down and tell them, "Look, I understand where you're coming from, and you want to be safe, but if we do what you're suggesting, we'll fall behind. We will have time to figure this all out in real time. We can pivot our efforts as the results come in."

For me as the leader, purpose became a tool I could use to reframe the decision-making process. With purpose, I could help them see why we needed to move faster than what they were used to. The ones who could find the overlap with their own purpose stayed. The ones who couldn't left.

Whether you're in leadership or not, you always have the choice to set personal goals that complement the organization's objectives.

For instance, let's say part of your purpose in life is to set up your children for a better education than what you had. You find the best private school in town and calculate the tuition. You then use this mark as part of your sales goal. The company quota may be ten deals a month, but you know that for you to fulfill your personal purpose, you need twelve deals a month. By fulfilling your personal purpose, you also fulfill the company's purpose to serve more people. And by default, you're also doing the extra that will build your credibility and opportunities.

You can also choose to seek out projects that resonate with your own personal values. Do the extra that allows you to do more of what you love in the role. Anyone can get comfortable doing the same task every day and achieving the same results. But underdogs don't need comfort. They need the challenge.

With both approaches, you make the choice to bring alignment to your purpose and the company's mission. You may never be 100 percent in sync with a company's mission until you have your own. Nor do you have to let the company's mission overtake your personal identity.

However, when you choose to focus on what you love about your work and to do the extra, then you can often create the necessary alignment. And when enough people notice the value you're bringing, then you gain influence in how the company's purpose and mission are being fulfilled.

Managing Mission Misalignment

Throughout your professional journey, you need to regularly revisit your personal purpose and how it complements the mission and purpose of the organization you're working for. Always be ready to course correct rather than slip into complacency.

If you find that you and the company are drifting apart, then you can adjust your effort accordingly, whether that's to bring yourself into more alignment with the company's purpose—or whether you need to keep your eyes open for the next opportunity.

If you choose to stay on the company's payroll because you're not ready to make a move, then do not allow your efforts to slip. Even when the seas are rough, make sure you stabilize the ship first, or the takeoff will go poorly.

Next, evaluate your foundation. When you see a gap forming between your purpose and the company's purpose, ask yourself what the cause is. Have your values changed? Are you living up to them? Or have the values of the company changed, and you're moving opposite directions?

For instance, is geography still a variable for you? If you're living near your support system, then you have a stronger foundation compared to picking up and leaving. It's one thing to move if you're alone, but if you have a spouse and children, moving to a new area with no support system is asking for stress.

Consider the industry you're in. Is the misalignment being caused by an industry shift? If so, then perhaps you need to consider leaving the industry. Look at the competitors and what they are doing for validation.

Before you make a drastic change, you have to isolate where the problem is. If you like the work environment but not the industry, then pick up and move. If neither the environment nor the industry is the problem, then you need to begin learning the skills for the role you want. And if the opportunity for such a role is lacking where you are, then prepare yourself to leave. Sometimes if you want to move up, you've got to move out.

Don't allow misalignment to go unchecked. Recognize it early and take proactive steps to either close the gap through your efforts—or when necessary, to seek out the environment with a mission more closely aligned to your purpose. Remaining in misalignment is a one-way ticket to burnout and missing your next opportunity.

Reflaction—The Underdog's Mission Statement

Purpose gives you something to fight for. Underdogs wield their purpose as both shield and sword. They empower every action with purpose.

Whether you're an underdog or not, adopt the underdog approach. Consistently take yourself to the ER by looking at your effort and results. Everything else is a distraction.

Victim mentality sees everything as "the world is against you." Underdog mentality sees everything as "you must do more and do better than what the world expects of you."

Where victims drop out, underdogs dig in. They work harder than anyone else, which changes how they are seen. They go from being viewed as underdogs to being seen as the top dog.

CHAPTER 12: **ALIGNING PERSONAL PURPOSE AND COMPANY MISSION**

Though I've been an underdog multiple times in my life, I don't feel like one anymore. My identity is no longer defined by the challenges facing me but by the challenges I've overcome. Yet because I chose the underdog approach, I still gravitate toward underdog challenges, like my venture Cadrenal Therapeutics. Tecarfarin is an underdog drug, a thousand-to-one long shot compared to a Big Pharma blockbuster. But it's greatly needed because Big Pharma prefers big blood-thinning markets.

In general, Americans root for underdogs. Just look at the sports stories we gravitate toward—Rudy Ruettiger and Notre Dame, Joe Namath and the Jets, Herb Brooks and the Miracle on Ice team. These are stories where weaknesses were not ignored. Rather, they are stories where the power of purpose overrode the weaknesses.

Likewise, spend some time identifying your underdog traits. What are your perceived weaknesses in terms of your work? It could be lack of experience. It could be your cultural background. It could be a toxic boss or lack of opportunity. Before you can wield the underdog mentality, you have to be able to acknowledge your underdog traits and deal with any insecurities.

Now that you are in the mind frame of an underdog, you can do the most important piece of this exercise:

Develop your personal purpose statement.

You wouldn't believe the difference it makes when you take an idea out of your head and put it into words. It changes your perspective and provides a new sense of empowerment.

If you feel stuck on where to start, look up some of the personal purpose statements for your Admirables. Look at the mission statements for some of your favorite brands and get a feel for how they are formulated. Then block off some time to create your own.

Don't worry—no one else needs to see it. You don't have to tattoo it on your body or put it on your résumé—though having a personal *why* on your résumé can certainly help you stand out from the crowd.

You don't have to write it in stone either. You're allowed to upgrade your purpose as needed. But by creating your own purpose-driven mission statement through the lens of the underdog mentality, you will better envision your success. You'll be one step closer to taking your definition of success and putting it into action. You'll have your creed as a citizen of Underdog Nation.

Purpose must be more than a buzzword. For underdogs, purpose always drives action. And when you zero in on how your purpose empowers your journey to success, it won't just transform your life—it will transform your world.

CONCLUSION

The ER Approach in Action

In all the rounds of golf I've played, I've only had one hole-in-one. The sport is an addicting mental grind. You do the same motion, over and over, the same effort—but you don't always get the same results. The ball goes in the bunker. It goes into the water. It's a game of great precision, where the slightest microscopic variable in your swing can send the ball out into the woods—or right into the cup.

While I always enter an amateur competition envisioning myself as the winner, I don't win most of the time. Even so, I shake the winner's hand at the end and congratulate them on their success, because even at the amateur level, we all know how difficult the game is.

What I've noticed about my own game, though, is that my skills never improved from taking lessons or hitting a thousand balls at the driving range. I only improved once I started playing in more competitions. Can you learn from watching the pros play? Sure. Can you learn from taking lessons? Of course. But the real improvement in my effort and results didn't occur until I experienced repetition in competition and overcame the nervousness that comes with competing.

Likewise, you can read all the books in the world—including this one—and they won't do anything for you if you don't put what you learn into action. Until you start taking action when there are real stakes, you won't see any difference.

As I said in the beginning, this is why mindset is not enough. You must have action. You might not achieve the results you hope for at first, but you will learn, adjust, and continue forward.

That's the power of the ER approach. Instead of worrying about a thousand different factors, you zero in on your effort and results. Like my old CO said during mission briefings: "In zone, on time." Life is complicated enough. Your formula for success doesn't have to be.

Every lesson here boils down to those two elements of your effort and results. If you will focus on the E and R, taking individual accountability for both, then you will automatically be ahead of 90 percent of people out there who are simply coasting through life, doing the minimum, and complaining that they "never got their shot."

In golf, we have four main types of clubs: drivers and woods for longer-distance shots, irons for shorter precision shots, sand wedges to get out of those pesky bunkers, and putters to deliver the ball to its final destination with accuracy. Likewise, within the ER approach, you have the four other approaches to help you along the way. Different scenarios will require a different approach:

- Commitment (your drivers/woods)
- Confrontation (your irons)
- Course Correction (your sand wedge)
- Credibility (your putter)

With these four types of clubs in your metaphorical golf bag, you can deliver the ball from where you are now to where you want to be.

CONCLUSION

It won't be perfect. A gust of wind might carry you off into the rough. You might get lost in the pond and have to take a drop. But get back in play. And every so often, everything aligns the way it should, and you'll sink the ball on the first shot. Just don't ever walk off the course because of a lack of result!

No matter which club you're using, you must have purpose in your swing. When a golfer isn't fully committed to his or her swing, it never goes well. There's no disguising the lack of commitment when they pull up short instead of following through.

If the shot doesn't go the way you hope, don't throw your club or drop out of the tournament. Don't pout or make excuses. You only improve by staying in the game. That bad hole will teach you a lesson if you keep your mind open to learn. And if you can reframe the negative experience to focus on what you've learned, then the next one will go much better.

With this in mind, bring together the other lessons you've learned along the way. Revisit the twelve reflactions throughout the book and review them on a regular basis so you don't grow complacent:

- **Identify Your Admirables.** What can you learn from the purpose they displayed? What are the mistakes and wins in their lives you can apply to your own?

- **The Pivot.** How are you adapting to circumstances and addressing your perceived weaknesses? Have you adopted go/no-go decision-making?

- **The 20/80 Rule.** What is the 20 percent of your job you love? How can you grow that 20 percent to maximize your influence?

- **Good FOMO.** What should you be afraid of missing out on? What is the extra you need to do to create the right opportunities?

- **Patient Preparation.** What are you doing to prepare yourself? Are you putting in the work to grow?

- **Give a Damn.** How is your EQ? How do you need to be growing your emotional intelligence?

- **Reframe Negative Experiences.** Are you wallowing in regret? Or are you using negative experiences as lessons and motivation?

- **Support Systems.** Who do you have around you to support you and help you grow? Who do you still need in your support system to help you reach the next level?

- **Your Resilience Plan.** Have you created a resilience plan? Have you built in the necessary resources to be your safety net in the face of a setback?

- **Fake It 'til You Make It.** Are you envisioning where you want to be so you can take the required efforts to achieve those results? Are you creating confidence and credibility?

- **Find Your Boat.** Have you identified the core values that will keep you constant in the midst of challenges and change?

- **The Underdog's Mission Statement.** Are you looking at your circumstances from the view of an underdog? Have you defined your purpose-driven mission statement?

The beauty of the Effort and Results approach is you don't need to have the same experiences as anyone else to apply it. You only need the honesty and accountability to take ownership of your effort and results. When that is paired with purpose and commitment, then you will unleash the underdog within. It's the ER within the undERdog.

Remember, no one else gets to define success for you. And you're allowed to redefine success as you go through your journey. The ten-year-old who wanted to follow in his dad's footsteps to be a pilot would have never imagined his life would go from fleeing a war to ringing the bell on Wall Street.

Looking ahead to the future, I realize there will always be unknowns. Even with my current venture, Cadrenal, there are so many factors outside of my own efforts, so many results I cannot control. But what I can control is to wake up each day with gratitude, recenter on my purpose, and do the extra.

No special talent is required. You can do the same. Rain or shine, grab your clubs and join the game. Whether it takes you one swing or ten, keep swinging. Your effort and results will carry you to the hole.

In a world where most people settle for lives shaped by chance and complacency, commit to being the underdog. Zero in on your effort and results, and success will follow. Because there are no losers in the Underdog Nation.

ABOUT THE AUTHOR

Quang X. Pham is the founder and CEO of Cadrenal Therapeutics, a biopharmaceutical company developing tecarfarin, a novel blood thinner for patients with rare cardiovascular conditions. He is the first American of Vietnamese heritage to become a US Marine Corps aviator and lead a biotech IPO on Nasdaq (CVKD). He is also the author of *A Sense of Duty: Our Journey from Vietnam to America* and has received the EY Entrepreneur of the Year® award. A graduate of UCLA, he is a popular speaker and lives in Florida with his family. For more information, visit www.quangxpham.com.

www.ingramcontent.com/pod-product-compliance
Lightning Source LLC
Jackson TN
JSHW021045090325
80368JS00001B/1/J